# The Sniper's Guide to Leadership

*How to become an effective leader without gunning down your staff*

# Mélanie Hope

sniperleader.com

The Sniper's Guide to Leadership
How to become an effective leader without gunning down your staff.
Copyright © 2014 Hope Speaking, LLC
HopeSpeaking.com

Cover drawing by James Mosier. Layout and design by StormKatt Productions. All graphics and illustrations are original works and sole property of the author.

Books may be purchased in bulk for educational, business, fundraising, or sales promotional use. For information on discounts and terms, please email books@hopespeaking.com

Paperback ISBN: 9781477642467
Kindle  ASIN: B0O2T63IS
BISAC: BUS071000 BUSINESS & ECONOMICS / Leadership

10 9 8 7 6 5 4 3 2 1

Las Vegas, NV

# Dedication

To every clueless boss who can't figure out why no one gets anything done correctly or on time.

To every desk jockey, cubicle dweller, and code monkey who wishes his or her boss had a clue.

Let's meet in the middle, shall we?

# CONTENTS

# INTRODUCTION

Snipers get a bad rap, particularly since the Press seems determined to label any crazy with a gun a "sniper." The fact is that an authentic, qualified sniper is a very intelligent, incredibly patient, superior marksman who has been highly trained. His job is to take out a specific target, yes, but with the ultimate outcome of saving many, many more lives.

There are actually a few qualities that a good sniper and a good leader share:

- Each knows his job well
- Each also knows everyone else's jobs
- Both have unlimited patience
- Both use highly specialized tools

If you lie in wait, lining up that perfect shot, just itching for that one employee to make a move so that you may pull the trigger and take him down, then you are not doing your job as a leader. You are sabotaging your team and every member therein. This is quite the opposite of a sniper's gig. The sniper lines up his shot in order to save his entire team – and he never aims at his own teammates.

Are you really a nice person and would never consider doing such a thing? That's too bad. Your incompetence has your team thinking otherwise. It doesn't matter if you don't actually have your finger on the smite button. If everyone who works for your THINKS you do, the results are the same.

As a manager, you do not have the luxury of suiting up in camouflage and keeping to yourself in stoic silence. While this works for a sniper, it does not work for a leader.

1

# *WHY A GOOD SNIPER MAKES A BAD LEADER*

The most important part of a sniper's job is that he works alone (or at best, with a single spotter). He must know exactly when to take a shot, if he gets one, with no advice from or consultation with the rest of the players. This inherently makes him a bad candidate for management.

Leaders cannot work alone.

A sniper may have to lie completely still for many, many hours – maybe even days. He can't break for lunch or change his vantage. He cannot flit around asking folks how they're doing. He must remain completely still, waiting for that perfect moment.

Leaders cannot stay still.

A sniper is effective only because the target has no idea of his existence. If a sniper is seen, he is useless. In fact, he cannot tell anyone that he is a sniper, even when off-duty. He must protect his position and identity at all costs.

A leader cannot be invisible.

When a sniper is lining up his shot, he must completely clear his mind of anything else. He cannot sympathize with the target. He cannot think of whether he hurts its feelings or is sensitive to its cultural differences. He cannot see it as a person, or he won't be able to complete the task.

A leader must be empathetic.

Unlike a hunter, a sniper cannot change his mind and shoot at different prey, should something else yummier or easier to hit wander into his sight.

A leader must be flexible.

Everyone else depends on the sniper to do his job right, the first time, every time. In fact, there may only be one shot, period. The sniper cannot even consider the possibility of missing. He cannot run through scenarios with repercussions of his missing the shot. He cannot fail, or he will endanger countless others.

A leader must be able to fail.

When a sniper chooses his vantage, he must also consider his escape route. In many cases, this may be as important as the vantage itself – getting the hell out of there after the target is down.

A leader cannot run away from anything.

A sniper must be well-versed in not just ballistics, but wind speed and direction, barometric pressure and temperature, range of movement, optimal positioning, collateral damage assessment, and many, many other factors. He must run through all of these to line up a single shot, and he cannot focus on any other activity but that single shot.

A leader must be able to juggle.

A sniper must be able to exploit the weaknesses of his enemy. He must know his own and his team's weaknesses and be able to compensate for them.

A leader must focus only on the strengths of his team.

As you can see, being the type of leader that strengthens a team, motivates them to success, and coaches them to greatness takes a lot more skills than just following the numbers and being bossy.

It takes all of those soft skills that were ignored through the Industrial Age. Robots have replaced the assembly line workers, and now you've got to learn how to work with real people and lead them, rather than boss them.

We are in the Age of Knowledge now. Money is no longer a strong enough motivator to garner loyalty or even hard work. Luckily, you have in your hands a resource that will explain how to go from autocratic inefficiency to holistic incredibleness.

Read through Part 1, find yourself in one or some of the stories (don't worry, the names have been changed to protect the guilty), take notes, and then read on to Part 2 to learn how to change those sniper ways. You have more than just the ability to intimidate your team into compliance – you have the power to coach them to greatness.

# PART 1: ANATOMY OF A BAD BOSS

*Even though worker capacity and motivation are destroyed when leaders choose power over productivity, it appears that bosses would rather be in control than have the organization work well.*
*~ Margaret J. Wheatley*

If you find yourself constantly called on the carpet for your staff underperforming, please _do_ take it personally. As much as you want to blame Bob for turning in his reports late or Maybelle for never doing a spellcheck on her company-wide emails, if your staff stinks, it's _your_ fault. Plain and simple.

Is it fair that you should take all the blame all the time? You bet your sweet bippy! The truth is, your job is supposed to be hard. That's why you get paid the big bucks! If you don't like it, let go of that corporate ladder rung you're gripping for dear life and fall back to where you belong. There is no shame in not wanting to be a leader – if everyone wanted to be a leader, who would we lead? The only shame comes from deciding not to be a good leader and taking others down with you because you have made that decision.

Sometimes it's just too easy to assume that bad bosses are evil tyrants who hate their lives, their work, their employees, and themselves. It's a little too easy to forget that bosses are people, too. Perhaps you don't realize the effect you're having on your department. Maybe you simply don't recognize yourself as a bad boss.

Part of you must, though, or you wouldn't be reading this book. If someone gave it to you, consider it a mental breath mint. (No one just hands another person a breath mint out of the blue. If you're getting this as a gift, you *need* it.) Take it graciously with the understanding that their intention was to help you. Turn to the highlighted or bookmarked page and read what others see in you.

Don't worry, with just a little insight you can – and will – improve your attitude, your aptitude, and approach. We'll start with a little tough love.

Following are the sniper's qualities that do not translate well into a good leader, mentor, or coach. Keep in mind that these examples are based on real stories about *real* bosses. Yes, even the burning building actually happened. Are you one of these bosses?

# *YOU TRY TO WORK ALONE.*

*No man will make a great leader who wants to do it
all himself or get all the credit for doing it.*
~ Andrew Carnegie

Angel was excited to be able to utilize her new accounting degree at her entry-level job. She figured she'd soak up as much knowledge as possible and, with that experience, eventually move up the ranks in the accounting world. She was willing to start with the basics, even though she was capable of so much more. Unfortunately, her boss wouldn't let her do much more than filing. "Every time she had a project for me, I would barely get started on it before she'd take it back. If I asked any questions, it was like I was a huge inconvenience. She kept saying it was easier for her to just do it herself than to explain it to me."

Let's face it, if you want something done correctly, you have to do it yourself, right?

Wrong.

If you truly believe that you must do everything yourself, then you are not a leader at all. A real leader is in the business of ensuring everyone else can and wants to do his or her job. If you are doing it all yourself, it is only because you have failed to delegate.

What stands in the way of you leading your team? Here are some reasons that bosses find themselves alone a lot:

## NO ONE CAN DO IT AS GOOD AS YOU

> *I am learning that perfection isn't what matters. In fact, it's the very thing that can destroy you if you let it.*
> ~ Emily Giffin

Sebastian was new in the department, but he had a lot of experience and at every prior position was lauded for learning fast. If his manager told him how to fix something, he'd fix it and never make the same mistake again. That was how he learned: By doing.

The problem was that his new manager, Kate, wouldn't let him fix anything. "She'd send me an email with a bulleted list of the things she had to correct – but never actually let me do it! This was her version of training. It only took once of not doing it to her standards, and she'd never let me do it again. Pretty soon, she was doing all of my reports and hers, and I later found out that she did most of our department's reports. Several of us had nothing left to do but busywork. If she didn't trust us, why did she hire us?"

There are three things woefully wrong with being the type who cannot delegate. First, you end up overworking yourself. Second, you take any pride or joy away from those who want to do good work or learn new things. Third, you set yourself up for others to take advantage of your illness, much like the teenage boy who purposely drops dishes so that his mother never asks him to do them again.

You have a team for a reason. They will make you look good, but only if you give them a chance.

## YOU WANT THE GLORY

> *It is amazing what you can accomplish if you do not
> care who gets the credit.*
> ~ Harry S. Truman

Randy joked about his lonely job in Accounts Payable, since he was the only person there. His job was to match, code, and enter the bills to be paid. Every Friday, he would print checks and send them out for signatures. Once returned, he would match checks and mail them out. While the Controller, Debra, was on vacation, Steve, the floor manager, approached Randy on a Friday morning and asked if it were possible to get his expense report paid that day. "I told him I'd make sure it made this week's batch, and I did. I thought I was doing a good thing. When Debra came back, she chewed me out for telling Steve that I handled such things. I didn't understand why she was so upset. She told me that I had no right to tell anyone who did what – that, as far as anyone else was concerned, she did it all, and I was never to tell another person anything that I did in HER office."

This is one of the most difficult points a boss must digest: Even if you *did* do it all, you owe it to your team to give them credit. If you're not willing to work with a team, then why have a team at all? If you really did do it all, then fire every last person under you and reproduce those results all by your little self. It won't be long until you go bonkers or burn yourself out completely.

# YOU'RE A DIVA

> *I'd love to be a diva. But I'd then have to send so many*
> *apology notes for my abhorrent behavior.*
> *~ Amy Adams*

Yoko was an administrative assistant to the CFO of a mid-sized company. The CFO, Stacey, obviously was a diva. "We called Stacey 'The Devil Wears Pull-ups' because she was such a tyrant and a baby at the same time," confesses Yoko. "She would get personally offended if anyone got kudos for anything, and once threw a tantrum because I got an award. I mean – literally – stamping, yelling, and tossing insults at me. She announced to the whole office that I didn't deserve it. No one took her seriously."

If you can't get them all to love you, they should, at the very least, fear you. They should all know how you take your coffee, what your dog's name is, and whether they are allowed to wear your favorite shade of red on Thursdays so they won't clash with your tie. They should walk on eggshells around you, bow to your whims, and even avoid you if they can. You are better than they are, right? You DEMAND that respect. Now. Period. Screw everyone else and their petty opinions.

The problem with this elitist attitude is that you establish yourself as a simple-minded jerk. No matter your skills or background, people will take you for face value, and your staff will assume that you got your position by luck or connections, rather than skill or experience. No amount of huffing and puffing will change that. You have no true respect.

What happens when you move up the ranks but are unable to create any loyalty? Think about it. You may not mind being lonely at the top, but you will mind losing profits, clients, and the best people.

# YOU'RE GOOD AT STAYING STILL.

*Progress is impossible without change, and those who cannot change their minds cannot change anything.*
*~ George Bernard Shaw*

Larry couldn't believe it when the owner forced him to delete his database, "He said that we've done our expenses on paper since the company was founded, and that is the way we'd be doing it until he sold it. He didn't even care that what I created was way more accurate, faster, and would have saved him more than $1,000 a week just in returns."

Things are just fine the way they are. Why change? In fact, why do anything at all? You've been successful enough doing things one way. In fact you may resent those that want to make changes – what do they know?

They know that if you stay still, you stagnate. Ever smelled stagnant water? Ick. The business world has changed drastically in a very short time. It shows no sign of slowing down, either. You better keep up!

# YOU ARE SHORTSIGHTED

> *If you don't know where you are going, you'll end up*
> *someplace else.*
> *~ Yogi Berra*

"The owners of the company I worked for were so interested in creating more profit that they started creating products that rivaled those of companies they had contracts with," tells Jorge.

"They incentivized the employees with parties, cash, and days off. Everyone was so excited about the incentives that they rallied against the middle manager that spoke out about the bad business practices. His boss went on and on about how he built the company from nothing and he knew what he was doing. He did know about basic business, but he didn't know anything about long-term growth and competition. In less than one year, we all lost our jobs. A company that once traded for $32 a share ended up bankrupt and not worth a penny."

If you only care about profits or marking off boxes on your goal sheet, then you've missed the point. Short-term gain is really no gain at all. Think of it as an athlete on steroids. He might win a game or finish a marathon or even win multiple races or several gold medals – but then what? If he isn't caught, he's still only good for so long, and then his health fails. He's a one-trick pony who cheated for even that one trick.

Do you believe that you can ride on the glory of only one win for your entire career? Do you cheat your team out of a productive work environment by focusing only on artificial goals and immediate profits?

Wouldn't you rather create an environment where you and your team can repeat good results over and over? It's only going to happen if you think a little farther ahead than what you're thinking now.

## YOU KNOW EVERYTHING THERE IS TO KNOW

> *Leadership and learning are indispensable to each other.*
> ~ *John F. Kennedy*

"Natty would send us to training seminars, but never go herself," says Meghan. "She said she had been a manager long enough that she pretty much knew it all. Weird. You'd think that if she knew it all, she'd be better at what she did. We were always having to clean up her messes because she didn't even know how to do simple things that the rest of us did – like work the phones."

Are you so happy with your training that you think you're done forever? It's pretty clear by the title of this section that this is a bunch of bunk. NEVER, ever, ever stop reading, learning, growing, and thinking. There are millions of leadership seminars and books out there because the topic never gets stale. It's not the same world it was when you entered the workforce, and people's outlooks and attitudes are changing every day, but basic, effective communication is still the same. We learn new things from both old and new sources, so keep reading.

Think about it, would half of cable TV be reruns if there weren't anything valuable the second time? Would anyone read the bible or their favorite novel more than once if they didn't rediscover something or see it in a different light? There are reasons so many versions of the same basic message exist – people learn in different ways at different times.

Whenever you try to convince others that you're smarter than they are, you conclusively prove that you aren't. Get out there and improve yourself.

# *YOU ARE INVISIBLE.*

> Behind the ostensible government sits enthroned an invisible government owing no allegiance and acknowledging no responsibility to the people.
> ~ *Theodore Roosevelt*

"We knew our supervisor's name was Andrew," confesses Rita, "but only a couple of us actually knew what he looked like. He sent tons of emails, left messages, and once in a while would schedule a meeting, only to phone it in. It became a joke. Who was this guy, and what the hell were we supposed to be doing? I swear, the only time we ever saw him was during annual reviews which was stupid, because how could he possibly know how well we were doing?"

Do you keep the details of your position so close to the vest that your team doesn't think you actually do anything at all? Are you so concerned with meetings and protocol that you haven't learned what your staff's jobs are, how to do them, or even where they fit into your position? You may think that you are very busy and important – and you may well be – but if you aren't familiar with your own staff and their struggles and strengths, then what are you there for at all?

## YOU DON'T ESTABLISH YOURSELF AS ALPHA

> *Everybody has a plan until they get punched in the face.*
> ~ Mike Tyson

Jeremy is still uncertain of his role in his department, "My manager, Kevin, is a great guy, but he doesn't really lead us. In fact, I think most of the people in the department think I'm the manager, since they all come to me with their questions and issues. I've been here almost as long as Kevin, and I do a lot more than he does, so I might as well be the boss. I'm just a little pissed that I don't get Kevin's pay."

Meanwhile, Kevin admits, "I wish that Jeremy would ask me before he lets someone leave early or take a day off. It's like he doesn't know who the boss is!"

Have you ever heard of the alpha dog principle? It doesn't matter if you've never owned a dog or even if you don't like dogs, this basic principle applies to human relations. Every team needs to establish an alpha leader. Typically, they have a title such as manager, supervisor, team leader, or senior.

When in the wild, a pack of dogs will determine the leader, or alpha dog. In your home, you are the pack leader. A dog will look up to you to see what acceptable behavior is and is not. If you do not establish yourself as the one who determines this, one of two things will happen:

1. The dog will become upset or anxious, as he does not know what role he should fill.
2. The dog will look around for an alpha and, finding none, determine he must be it.

Neither of these responses benefits you or the dog.

If you try to establish yourself as alpha by being harsh, punitive, or abusive, you will be met with aggression, anxiety, stress, and more bad behavior. You are establishing yourself as a bully, not a true alpha.

In the wild, an alpha establishes himself as the pack leader by demonstrating clear direction and showing he is strong and confident. He leads his team with structure and purpose and without tension or anger.

See? This is your goal as a leader of humans.

## YOU'RE TOO BUSY

> *Beware the barrenness of a busy life.*
> ~ Socrates

Frank worked for a demanding consulting firm where he and his teammates noticed that their team leader was always too busy to actually be a leader. Does this sound familiar?

"Tony said that he had an open-door policy, which meant that his door was always closed and locked with the 'Open-Door Policy' plaque hanging on it. We rarely saw the guy, and we didn't have a clue what he actually did. All we know is that sometimes he'd pull us into a meeting to describe some project that we had to work late to clean up – that we had no idea existed until it was a crisis. When we'd ask why he didn't get it to us sooner, he'd sigh and say that he was just too busy. Too busy to do his job?"

Frank's team needed a leader, but the one with the title wasn't available. Was he too busy, or was he afraid of leading?

If you find that you are too busy to be a leader, then you are missing the point. The first thing an effective leader does is delegate. When you delegate work to your team, you empower them to do what they do best: Support the organization as a whole.

A little bit of delegation goes a long way to freeing up the time you need to mentor your team to victory. If you want to be an effective coach, you can't do it by playing all of the positions yourself.

## YOU ARE SURPRISED BY OFFICE DRAMA

> *You can't save others from themselves because those who make a perpetual muddle of their lives don't appreciate your interfering with the drama they've created. They want your poor-sweet-baby sympathy, but they don't want to change.*
>
> ~ Sue Grafton

"We were in the middle of a routine meeting, when all of a sudden, Sophia jumped out of her chair, screamed that she was sick of Evan's crap, and ran off sobbing," recounts Michael, a regional VP of Marketing. "What the hell? After much coaxing and a meeting with HR, it turned out that there was an ongoing issue between these two, even though they had worked on several successful projects together. Sophia swears that she had mentioned this to me, and that I hadn't done anything. Well, I remember her saying something, but I didn't think it was that big of a deal. She's always complaining about something."

Unless we're talking about your own birthday party, you should never be surprised at the office. You must be fully aware of the tensions and issues amongst the staff. If not, where have you been? If you aren't talking to your team or don't know even a little bit about their working lives, you've ignored one of the basic principles of leadership. Plug in! Try this easy, five-point plan for office drama:

1.  If a team member approaches you with an issue, listen. Let them vent first, and then ask them directed questions to get the background. Is this a tattletale seeking your approval, or a real issue? (See: "You bow to the Tattletale")

2. If this is an issue that they cannot solve on their own, take action right away. Letting things fester or writing them off as insignificant is a recipe for disaster.
3. Pull in both members. Talk to them.
4. Work with them to create a plan to resolve the issue. It could be anything from a simple apology to taking a class together.
5. Check in with both parties on a regular basis. Hold them accountable for their choices.

# YOU DO NOT LEAD BY EXAMPLE

*As a leader, your word is only as good as your last promise kept or broken.*
~ BJ Gallagher

Stan was mortified when he got the owner's expense report. "He had all of these crazy things from Las Vegas on it – from hotels and fancy dinners to strippers (honest!), booze, and even a motorcycle. OK, sure, the motorcycle had been custom-painted with our logo on it, but really? Plus, everyone in the office knew full well that this wasn't even a business trip. This was his honeymoon. I don't care if you do own the damn company, that is not ethical or legal, and I told him so. He told me he did it all the time, all the execs did, too. I told him I'd been sending those back, too, because I needed explanations for each charge of how they related directly to the business. Lost my job over that one, but he ultimately lost the company and is still in trouble with the IRS. I guess I dodged a bullet there."

Forget that the media keeps screaming about how we should overlook the indiscretions of dirty politicians – character *does* count! Your only job, truly, is to set the example for the rest of your crew to follow. The rest is just paperwork.

Be on time. Do what you say you're going to do, give a rat's hindquarters about those "little" issues. Be honest. Cultivate, motivate, celebrate! That really is your job.

Being a manager is supposed to be difficult – that's why you get paid more. Your title does not automatically guarantee respect, you have to EARN that. Otherwise, you'd just get a medal or tassels to hang from your sleeves.

No, instead, you are entrusted with better hours, more pay, and sometimes even a closer parking spot. People are supposed to look up to you. Be a person worthy of that respect and they'll follow you anywhere.

If you want passion, ethics, or hard work from your employees — then you must be passionate, ethical, and hardworking!

# *YOU'RE ANYTHING BUT EMPATHETIC.*

*When you show deep empathy toward others, their defensive energy goes down, and positive energy replaces it. That's when you can get more creative in solving problems.*
~ *Stephen Covey*

Hank remembers the snowstorm from hell, "We were completely snowed in and worried about our families. Most of us had no clue how we'd get home, much less how we'd get into work the next day if it didn't let up. Christine went berserk and started threatening us with our jobs if we didn't come in the next day. Between her threats and our families, we didn't get a thing done all day."

Ugh! Aren't you sick of the whining and crying of your staff? What do they want, a shrink's couch in your office? If only they would just quit with their attention-getting ways and act like grownups, you might actually get something done around here.

Or, perhaps, if they just knew you gave a damn about them as human beings, they'd want to work for you. Your staff is not composed of robots. They have human feelings and ailments. Unless you can learn to be empathetic, you will always be painting yourself as an unfeeling enemy, not a leader.

This does not mean that you must dish out hot, fluffy pity by the plateful – quite the opposite! Pity does not build up an individual; it only makes him or her more dependent.

## YOU ARE A COUNSELLOR

*It's a mistake to confuse pity with love.*
*~ Stanley Kubrick*

"Philip was a great listener," June recalls of her former boss. "I'd see poor Karen go in there, day after day and just unload on him. She always had so much going on in her life that it was no surprise when he finally had to let her go. We all felt sorry for her, but she just went on and on."

Philip failed Karen.

Believe it or not, there really isn't a fine line between empathy and sympathy. When you are sympathetic with someone, you may feel with them, but you will never understand them. It can easily slip into pity, or at the very least, you end up being their counsellor through times bad and worse, and then there is nothing left to do but discipline them back into line.

What you don't get is any work done.

The truth is, your goal is to move *away* from the disciplinarian/counsellor mode and *toward* being more of a coach. This means being empathetic (not sympathetic) and ultimately holding them accountable for their choices.

Empathy means "feeling into" or understanding the person. It's the old 'walk a mile in their moccasins' principle. If you feel your staff is being whiny or looking to you to be their counsellor, put yourself in their position. Are they lacking a leader?

## YOU MISUNDERSTAND RESPECT

> *Always treat your employees exactly as you want*
> *them to treat your best customers.*
> ~ Stephen Covey

Gina recalls her first boss, a manager at a fast food restaurant, "This guy thought he was so important. He wasn't much older than the rest of us, but he had a title, so he'd expect us to call him 'sir.' He would talk down to us like we were scum – I mean, the little idiot probably made like 10 cents more than us – but he was so excited about being in charge that he became a tyrant. His favorite thing in the world was writing us up for every little thing. He spent more time doing that than anything else. We all thought he was a joke. He didn't last long, thank God."

Respect is granted, not given. What does this mean? In order to get respect, you must earn it. Any tight-fisted dictator knows that, while you may beat some form of fear out of your constituents, you will never have true respect and an overthrow is always imminent.

At that point, you have to constantly oppress your team to keep them in line. How effective can that be?

Another key point that many leaders overlook: You must show respect to everyone by whom you want to be respected. This is such a fundamental concept that it is true with dogs and children, too. They learn respect by being respected. You cannot beat a child or a dog into anything but fear. Fear is not respect. You cannot badger your employees into any form of respect, either. You must earn it.

## YOU TALK AT, NOT WITH YOUR STAFF

> *Think like a wise man but communicate in the language of the people.*
> ~ *William Butler Yeats*

Charles enjoyed the freedom of his job, so he felt the daily lectures were just part of the price he had to pay.

"Every morning, we had what Misty called a "stand up" meeting. I know she got it out of a book somewhere, but I'm not sure she read the whole book. Basically, it was 30 minutes of us standing around her desk while she told us everything that we needed to fix and everything we needed to finish that day...or else. No one asked any questions or got any actual feedback. Everything was very general. She'd end it with, "OK, team? Let's do it!" Then, we'd all go back to our cubes and just do whatever we thought we were supposed to do until tomorrow's lecture."

Brianna's supervisor took it one step farther: "Jacob would come to our desks and berate us. Sure, he made it sound all fluffy with things like, "I really feel that you would do better if you'd just (fill in the blank)," but it was mostly condescending nonsense that didn't motivate or help. Plus, if we asked a question, he'd just shake his head like we were stupid and walk away."

If you are only communicating one way, then you are not actually communicating, you're lecturing. Think back to your childhood when you got a good finger-shaking from an adult. Fun? Motivational? I didn't think so, did you? Why would you inflict that on anyone – especially if you want to get any work done?

## YOUR STAFF FEARS ANNUAL REVIEWS

*If you use an annual review cycle, you aren't getting
feedback at the same pace that you need to adapt and
change the business.*
~ Fred Wilson

Marcus ended up quitting his job because of his annual review. "I felt it was just a tool to demotivate me and make me feel like crap all the time. No matter what I did, it was wrong – but I never knew it until the end of the year. Why couldn't someone help me along the way?"

I call annual reviews "anal reviews" because of where it feels you may be pulling your insights. If you find that writing these things is difficult – even painful – it means that you haven't been communicating effectively with your staff. Nothing should ever be a surprise on any performance review. That's why it's called a REVIEW.

If your staff doesn't see their performance the same way you do, it's because you have not effectively communicated with them. If think you have tried, then you are not speaking their language. It is still your fault. Your failure to communicate has led to an unproductive environment and a painful review process that only creates animosity.

Sheila was ambushed with an HR issue. "I actually lost my chance at a raise because of an incident that happened six months prior to my review. The worst part? I had absolutely no recollection of this incident. None. The girl who accused me of saying something racist reported me to HR, but never spoke to me. HR never spoke to me, just reported it to my boss. My boss never spoke to me, just wrote it up in my file so it would bite me in the ass later. I am not a racist. In fact, I wasn't even familiar with the term she said I used. Since I didn't know the woman, I asked HR if this woman was absolutely sure it was me at all. They looked it up and found that she didn't even work for the company anymore! I was told to quit trying to lie my way out of it. Out of what? I didn't do anything! If someone would have spoken to me six months ago, we could probably have resolved it back then."

Annual reviews have become a tool for the passive-aggressive, making them ineffective and a source of fear, rather than what they should be. In the real world, an annual review should simply be that: A review of the prior year and a way to set goals for the coming year. Have you lost touch with that definition? Has your staff?

Annual reviews so often focus on the negative that many are left wondering if they ever do anything RIGHT. Have you ever felt that way? Imagine being a student who gets papers back with nothing but red marks all over them, but no grade. Imagine being a child who is taught, over and over again, how to tie your shoes – but never told when you actually do it correctly. When do you celebrate? How do you know that a job is actually done correctly?

If no one ever tells you: You don't.

You can guess, but will you ever be confident in your conclusions?

If your employees don't know exactly what will be on their annual reviews, then you have not been leading them.

## YOU ENGAGE IN FAVORITISM

*Treat everyone fairly, not equally.*
*~ Minh Tan*

Brad was the golden child. He came on board with a very impressive resume and a glowing recommendation from his previous employers. "Brad got all of the challenges, the perks – even the first open parking spot," relays Jane, "He may have been good, but he wasn't that good. It got to the point that we all hated Brad. He was the boss's pet and he knew it. He walked on water. No matter what we did, it was measured by how Brad might have done it. The thing that really stunk was that, because Brad had snowed the boss so well, he was a total slacker. We all had to clean up Brad's messes."

Being a good leader is very much like being a good parent: you cannot pick favorites. Just like in any family, it will lead to distrust, unhealthy competition, even sabotage. But, please don't think you can treat your team like family! We'll talk about that pitfall in Part 2.

## YOU PLAY GAMES

> *Self-centered leaders manipulate when they move*
> *people for personal benefit. Mature leaders motivate*
> *by moving people for mutual benefit.*
> ~ *John C. Maxwell*

Do you manipulate, intimidate, or subjugate? Do you keep your team guessing and groaning about your latest policy, procedure, or predicament? Are you addicted to the soap opera that is your office? Are they ducking and dodging your dastardly deeds? You, my friend, are a game player.

Challa was heartbroken when she found out from her manager, Sharon, that she had been rejected for the leadership program. "Sharon was the one who introduced me to the idea," she recalls, "She even helped me with ideas for the essay portion of the application. When she told me I didn't make it, I was pretty upset. She said she was angry, too, and we had a long talk about the unfair politics in upper management. Later I found out that it was Sharon who advised the committee not to accept me. She told them that I was 'not management material.' What kind of game was she playing? I almost quit because of her."

You should not be the crank on the rumor mill. Motivation is not defined as pitting one person against another or one department against the other. Even if you try to define it as competition, it is not healthy competition.

Healthy competition encourages growth and striving for success. It stretches your boundaries and allows you to take calculated risks. When you are competing in a healthy way, you find yourself learning from and even helping your competitors.

Unhealthy competition focuses on the negative aspects of losing. You pay more attention to other people's successes and are motivated by their losses. It is fed by shame and overcoming those that are weaker than you. It destroys teams and builds resentment.

These games that you are playing are setting roadblocks in front of your top performers. If you continue to pit them against each other, you will lose them.

# *YOU ARE INFLEXIBLE.*

*Companies used to be able to function with autocratic bosses. We don't live in that world anymore.*
~ Rosabeth Moss Kanter

Jefferson tried to figure out why the research department had a 10-step method of verification with paper files, when it could have been consolidated into a 2-step electronic process that saved both time and money. "Heather just gave me a blank stare and told me they've always done it that way, and no one was going to change it. Man, you'd think we worked for the government or something! Seriously, why wouldn't they want to save money?"

The business world is one of constant flux. The old days of doing things simply for the sake of tradition are long gone. Yes, you may be in a place of power because you earned it – but that is not a one-shot deal. You have to continually learn, improve, and grow. This means that you must be flexible, not only with yourself, but with your staff.

Keeping an open mind is not a cliché. It is a necessity. If you cannot change with the times, you and your dead position will be left behind. Don't drag your team down with you.

## YOU WOULD ONLY HIRE YOURSELF

> *Diversity: the art of thinking independently together.*
> ~ Malcolm Forbes

Juan was the owner of a seemingly growing technical company. While it had a built-in clientele based on its tiny niche, it couldn't grow without a strong staff. But, every time Juan hired someone, he felt it was his personal mission to destroy their confidence. In fact, he told new hires that they would not be able to keep their jobs unless they were willing to lose confidence to his superior logic. This really stressed Victoria.

"As a survivor of domestic violence, confidence is a very important and difficult thing to cultivate," Victoria conveys, "Someone with my background cannot function without confidence, and being told by a tyrant that I should give it up sent me back to the days of cowering in the corner, hoping I'd survive the night. Juan treated me as if I didn't matter. I became his pet project because he didn't like that I actually maintained my confidence, no matter his insults or arguments. I worked very hard to get to where I was, but he simply would not relent.

"I told him that, while he saw no issue with using that kind of language around the staff, several, me included, saw it as quite offensive and even abusive. I don't care if he is the owner; he could really get in trouble for treating people that way.

Juan's answer? "If they don't think the same way I do, then I don't want them working here."

Victoria couldn't believe her ears, "When I asked if he meant that he wasn't interested in diversity and only wanted to hire people like himself, he said, 'Yes.' Well, that certainly explained the revolving door of employees. I was the next to go."

Juan knew that his way of doing things was very specific, and he was only interested in hiring those who completely understood his particular philosophy, quirks, and processes. He simply could not fathom that there was another way other than his way. He wanted to surround himself with people that thought and reacted like he did, and he wasn't interested in even trying to be sensitive to others.

Juan had fleeting success, but his business stagnated. All of that potential was wasted because Juan had to be right.

Much like Juan, you may believe that you are the best for the job, so if you have plenty of little yous running around, things can only get better, right?

Things might get more boring, certainly. But better? Only if you view better as static.

Who is your best friend? Who is your spouse? Who do you admire? Are these people all exactly like you? Chances are, they all have something about them that is delightfully different. Otherwise, you wouldn't grow.

Your staff should be even more wonderfully diverse.

## YOU MICROMANAGE

> *Any company that requires constant supervision is*
> *not a well-trained, well-managed, well-led company.*
> *~ Larry Winget*

"Ingrid had this thing with keeping tabs on us – like, to the point that we had to tell her if we were headed to the bathroom or she'd come looking for us," Carla writes. "She dictated everything from what color of highlighter we could use on our meeting notes to what size pictures we were allowed to post in our cubicles. She made us send all emails through her first, even internal ones. Even as salaried employees, we had to clock out for our pre-scheduled breaks and lunches. She monitored our conversations, to the point that if she were in a meeting, she'd appoint one of us to give her a report of the goings-on when she returned."

Do you want adults working for you? Then treat them as adults! If everyone stops working when you aren't around, then blame yourself for creating that kind of culture. Yes, your micromanaging has made your staff LESS productive. Plus, all that extra work has got to be driving you nuts.

People who feel appreciated and empowered will want to do their jobs well without you breathing down their necks. Encourage both aspects of teamwork and autonomy, and you will find that creativity and productivity soars.

## YOU DO NOT ALLOW QUESTIONS

*The art and science of asking questions is the source of all knowledge.*
*~ Thomas Berger*

Alyce worked in a busy pizzeria as an assistant manager. Her boss, the owner, was more of a dictator than a manager. "One night we smelled something terrible and were pretty sure there was something wrong with the ovens. We called him at home, but he said not to worry about it."

"Later, smoke started billowing out of the top, but again he said to leave things alone. He would not give us permission to turn off the ovens or, at the least, to call a repair company to look at it."

"As the night wore on, the smoke got worse – until we had to vacate the building. We called him from the parking lot and explained the situation. He screamed at me to leave him alone and get back to work. As we were talking, I saw flames shoot from the roof of the building! I told him what was happening and he threatened to fire me, then hung up on me."

"I ended up watching the building burn to the ground. The chimney had been clogged, which set the roof on fire. I guess I could have called the fire department earlier, since I would have lost my job either way, but why bother?"

While this is an extreme example, there are millions of stories out there of bosses who actually get upset with their staff members who deign to ask questions.

Why? What are you so afraid of?

Kimberly recalls the last conversation she had with her former manager, "I am one of those people who kind of needs to know why we do something so that I can both remember it and do it correctly. When I asked my manager why we filed our auto leases by due date, rather than by lease number so that we could find them easier, she said, 'because I said so,' and actually turned her back on me! I quit that same day. Even my mother never spoke to me that way."

If someone needs an explanation, they need an explanation. Don't take it personally. Embrace the opportunity to teach and coach that person in that area. An employee that is asking questions is an employee that desires to learn, and an open-minded, teachable employee is an incredible asset.

## YOU DON'T KNOW WHAT THEY ACTUALLY DO

> *We are all born ignorant, but one must work hard to*
> *remain stupid.*
> ~ *Benjamin Franklin*

"Nathan would wander around the office asking each of us each if everything was OK, and then wander back into his office and close the door," confesses Raul, "Most of us would just tell him we were fine to get rid of him. Honestly, the few times we tried to explain an issue, his eyes just glazed over as if he had no idea what we were talking about. We all knew we couldn't depend on him for advice about our jobs, it was actually a running gag throughout the department."

If you have no idea how to do the jobs you're managing or even what your employees are supposed to be doing, then you have some serious issues. This is sometimes seen as the opposite of micromanaging, but often leads to the twisted, messy path of babysitting gone wrong simply because you can't trust what you don't understand.

"Tim would bring us all into his office to discuss the last report run," states Esther, "He'd ask things like, 'Can you explain this deviation?' We did everything we could not to laugh when he said that because he had no idea what he was asking. Of course the numbers were going to be different month-to-month. That's the entire reason we run the reports!

"First, we tried explaining to him the trends and market fluxes. He sort of understood that, so we'd just run with variations of that each month. One month, the numbers went haywire because of a technical glitch – and we completely lost him. He had no idea what we actually did, and he had no background in coding or reporting. When we explained, in detail, what happened and how we'd have to fix it, he just closed his eyes and asked if we could explain the deviation. We said yes, and he dismissed us to go take care of it.

"Once we realized that we could use any technical terms we wanted and he'd let us out of the meeting, we just made stuff up every time. 'Oh, yeah, uh...the deviation was caused by the reverse hotmonister on the flux capacitor in the back end. We'll be able to repair that within the hour by backing up the Boolean forescore with a positive string of qwerty.' We had so much fun making up things that it became a sort of contest to see who could come up with the craziest."

Don't want the wool pulled over your eyes? Stop being a sheep. If you're in a leadership role, you have to at least know what you're leading. If this means getting some technical training, do it. You will make yourself more valuable both to your organization and to your team.

# *YOU ARE NOT ABLE TO FAIL.*

> *I cannot give you the formula for success, but I can give you the formula for failure, which is: Try to please everybody.*
> ~ Herbert Swope

Carolyn still laughs at the poster her boss kept in the break room. It was a picture of Apollo 13 with the words, "Failure is not an option."

"OK, stranded astronauts is the only situation in which I can imagine trying that philosophy – but real life? Give me a break. We failed all the time and something good always came of it."

Fail is a four-letter word that gets as bad rap as snipers do – and it's not fair. Failure is actually the most important part of learning and absolutely necessary for succeeding. A mindset that you are unable to fail leads to debilitating and sabotaging behaviors – never success. In fact, more teams are led to failure simply because their leader was trying to avoid it.

Failure is where things are improved, where communication is enhanced, and where innovation is born. Failure is never an ending – it is always an opportunity.

Inability to admit to failure is not the same as not failing. In fact, it takes failure to an all-new level it might never have reached.

Allowing – and admitting to – failure is allowing growth and ultimately success.

# YOU TRY TO GET EVERYONE TO LOVE YOU

*You can't run a popularity contest and be successful.*
*~ Ara Parseghian*

When Barry came to Thomas with a timing issue, Thomas responded by taking three reports off of Barry's plate and handing them over to Sue. When Sue was upset, saying that Barry was always pushing things off on her, Thomas reassigned them to Gene. Gene ended up in Thomas's office, outraged that he got more work at the last minute, when he had so much going on already. Soon, Barry's three reports and two of Gene's were handed over to Anna. Anna burst into tears, saying that Gene was rude to her, so Thomas had Anna swap desks with Sue, and asked her to take on Barry's reports. Thomas then tried to pass Gene's reports to Allen. Allen had already asked for a lighter load because he was going on vacation next week, so Thomas himself stayed late and worked Sunday to get Gene's reports done.

Sounds ridiculous, right? It's a true story – and it kept going around and around like that until everyone decided that Thomas was a marshmallow who couldn't make a single decision. Meanwhile, everyone got very confused as to what his or her reports were anymore.

The only way you can get everyone to love 100% of what you do is to either be dead or to turn yourself into a free ice-cream machine. An effective leader cannot make everyone happy all the time.

## YOU BLAME YOUR PREDECESSOR

> *We are taught you must blame your father, your sisters, your brothers, the school, the teachers - but never blame yourself. It's never your fault. But it's always your fault, because if you wanted to change you're the one who has got to change.*
> ~ *Katharine Hepburn*

Jayme loved her job as a business analyst, that is, until her manager, Vince, was promoted into another department. "Our new manager told us in his very first meeting that, 'Things will be a lot different from when Vince was in charge.' They sure were! He didn't understand the team dynamic and proceeded to spend the next year blaming everything that failed on Vince. He didn't accomplish a single thing except to blame Vince's policies for everything that went wrong. If anything, he just broke things and blamed the guy before him. We all applied for transfers within the year."

From dictator to president to fast food shift manager, as a new leader you believe that you have fantastic ideas to fix the mess left by your predecessor. How long can you coast on blaming the other guy before your staff completely loses faith in you?

No matter how much of a screw-up the previous manager may or may not have been, at some point you've got to let go of that excuse. You're in charge now. Who cares what the other guy did? You won't get very far if you are constantly looking in the rearview mirror. Sure, you may have some real messes to clean up, but at what point do you begin to take responsibility for your own actions?

Well, when did you accept the job?

Yup, that's the moment you became the leader, and that's the moment you accepted responsibility. That should be the moment you gave up blaming the other guy. It may not be easy – but you volunteered.

# *YOU RUN AWAY FROM TROUBLE.*

*A good leader is a person who takes a little more than
his share of the blame and a little less than his share
of the credit.*
~ John C. Maxwell

"Our team was in charge of creating the integrated reports that
the budget team used for the following year's budget," reports
Don, "...and that was it. We only crunched the numbers, we didn't
interpret them. At the annual meeting, when they announced
awards, we were booed! I was about ready to sock the guy next
to me when he said that, thanks to us, their budget was cut in
half. Turns out that any time someone questioned or complained
about funds, the budgetary committee would tell them to blame
us."

Blame is always a losing game. Being a leader means that you pass
the praise, take the blame. Think about it: Who do they interview
after a big game? The guy who made the winning goal, basket, or
run. Who do they interview after a major loss? The coach. Have
you ever seen a coach pass the buck? Not a good one. And,
obviously, not a winning one.

When you start pointing your finger (and it doesn't matter which
finger that might be), you are not directing the focus elsewhere.
In reality, you are showing your weakness. Blame is a fun game to
play, but it always reflects badly on the blamer – less so on the
blamed. Why? Because blaming someone else is just so *easy*. As
long as you can blame, you can abstain – from any actual leading.

## YOU THROW YOUR TEAM MEMBERS UNDER THE BUS

> *Unintelligent people always look for a scapegoat.*
> *~ Ernest Bevin*

Celeste tried to tell her supervisor, Marge, that the deadline needed to be pushed back, but Marge told her, "Suck it up and work harder."

"No amount of sucking up could have allowed me to finish that database in that short of time all by myself," Celeste said, "especially with all the other things on my plate. But Marge kept telling the higher-ups that everything was going fine. When the time came to turn over the project and I was about two-thirds of the way finished, she told them all that she'd been having 'issues' with me from day one. Yes, the 'issues' were that she blamed me for her inability to face reality!"

You're holding on to that corporate rung for dear life. You worked hard to be where you are, and no staffer's failure is going to set you back. If your superior approaches you with an issue, you'll start screaming out names as if strapped to a waterboard. It's in your best interest to protect yourself, so you ain't taking the blame for some insubordinate lackey. No siree. Once they know who is really at fault, you're off the hook, right?

Well, no. Someone will catch on, and the higher you climb on the backs of others, the farther your fall will be. Plus, who will support you if no one below you can trust you?

## YOU BEAT AROUND THE BUSH

*First learn the meaning of what you say, and then speak.*
~ *Epictetus*

"There have been some complaints about your attitude," Rachel told Jon, "and we're going to have to do something about it."

"Um...OK, what attitude? What complaints? Who is having issues with me? What do I need to change?"

"Well...you know, Jon. I like you, you're a great guy. Just...work on it, OK?"

"This woman drove me crazy," Jon recalls, "I think she thought she was helping us by being so vague, but it made everything impossible. Whenever we'd try to corner her, she'd come up with generalities that really didn't tell us anything. I bet she went home mad at her husband every night and told him that old thing about 'If you don't know, I'm not going to tell you.' We don't know! Tell us!!"

Being indirect or unclear is just another passive-aggressive way to piss people off and leave them assuming you have no spine. Say what you mean. Say it nicely, but say it already. Don't sugarcoat it, don't apologize for it, and please – for all that is holy – don't let it fester until it's caused irreparable damage.

## YOU PLAY BY TWO SETS OF RULES

> *Leadership is a potent combination of strategy and character. But if you must be without one, be without the strategy.*
> ~ Norman Schwarzkopf

Cathy got promoted to supervisor, which took her from hourly to salary exempt status. Since that day, she routinely came in 10-15 minutes late. She'd take two hour lunches and would never let anyone know where she was going when she disappeared for long breaks during the day. Everyone else in the department had to punch time cards, and Cathy made sure HR docked the pay of anyone that was late, even if it was a working lunch that went over.

"Cathy's idea of "exempt" was that she was exempt from any of the rules she set for the rest of us," recalls Sandy. "She often said it didn't matter what time she came in or left because she got paid the same regardless. Meanwhile, we all had to clock in and out and were docked and reprimanded for even being a minute late. We hated her. Whenever she was gone, which was a lot, we just goofed off."

When you set yourself above your team, you are really only setting yourself up to fail. Remember the alpha dog syndrome? They look to you to determine how to act. That means that everything you do is scrutinized. Your actions determine the attitude and expectations of your staff. Expecting something of them that you are unwilling or unable to do only breeds contempt. Do you arrive late and leave early, sit on stale emails, skip reports, or miss a meeting now and then? What makes you so special? How can you expect your team to care if you don't?

If you want respect and loyalty, you must be the example of what you want to see in your team.

# *YOU CANNOT JUGGLE.*

*The world cannot be governed without juggling.*
*~ John Selden*

Justine needed help reorganizing her team, but her manager couldn't deliver. "Oliver said that he had to focus on the expense report and wasn't able to think about anything else until the financials were done. Then, after that deadline, he said that he was working on training the new manager, so he couldn't answer my questions."

"The new manager and I had lunch together, and she told me that Oliver wasn't able to do much with her because he said he was focusing on the office move. This guy was so tunnel-minded! My team was in limbo for almost three months until he could clear everything and focus on us."

Multitasking is all the rage, yet it has been proven over and over to actually decrease productivity. Does this mean that you should only plod along with one idea or task at a time?

Absolutely not!

Any juggler will tell you that you focus on the ball in the air, not on the hand in which it will land. Watch the arc, not your hands. Also, don't reach up to grab it, let it come to you. Once the idea is firmly implanted, all it takes is learning new patterns and you can juggle as many balls as you want!

Juggling also means that there is some risk involved. You can't juggle a ball unless you let go of it for a while. And, you can't let go of a ball until you get hold of it in the first place.

If you want to get more done and build your team, get those tasks and ideas in the air! Then, let them land successfully in your hands.

## YOU ARE REACTIVE RATHER THAN PROACTIVE

*Procrastination is like a credit card: it's a lot of fun until you get the bill.*
~ *Christopher Parker*

Jayson works as a dealer in a busy Las Vegas casino. In the Vegas tradition, he and his fellow dealers engage in banter that includes slang names for certain cards, such as hockey sticks for a pair of sevens or sailboats for fours. A pair of eights might be called 'two snowmen' or 'two fat ladies.'

"One night Mitch pulled up two eights at the Blackjack table and announced that the player had two fat ladies. The next day, our boss told us that Mitch was fired because the player complained that she was offended by the term 'fat ladies.' He then proceeded to tell us that we were no longer allowed to use ANY slang terms on the job, ever. Seriously."

"Now people are complaining that they aren't having fun. They want the Vegas experience, not some watered down, politically correct pussyfoot version. They're going to other casinos where they can get it. Word is, layoffs are around the corner."

Do you make blanket policies in response to a single complaint? Do you have so many rules of conduct that your department's operations manual is heavier than that of the IRS tax code? Does it feel like you spend so much time cleaning up messes that you can never get any actual work done? Knee-jerk overcompensating is a sign that you are a reactive manager.

Unless you are a firefighter, you should not be in the business of putting out fires.

A leader must make the transition from being a victim to being in charge, and then take action. This is a conscious decision that many take for granted. At some point, you – the leader – must change from being reactive to proactive.

This means looking ahead and planning. This also means that you must empower each member of your team to make those decisions that must be made on the fly. If you're proactive, you're looking ahead, getting your team involved in the process, and focusing on outcomes.

# *YOU FOCUS ON YOUR TEAM'S WEAKNESSES.*

*With power comes the abuse of power. And where there are bosses, there are crazy bosses. It's nothing new.*
*~ Judd Rose*

"Forrest held a sales meeting for us after we'd had a pretty rough season," relays Russell. "We'd had three straight months of sales that were 3% below goal. It was a slow time of year, so this was actually not a bad decline. But Forrest didn't see it that way. He took the drop not as a minor, temporary thing, but as a threat to his own credibility. Throughout the meeting he called out – by name – those he dubbed 'My Slower Sellers.' He told them, right there in front of the rest of us, that their jobs were on the line, then told them he would be retraining them personally over the next month, since he couldn't trust them.

"Not only were the "Slower Sellers" humiliated, we were ALL embarrassed by his display. Our team no longer acted like a team; instead we paid far too much attention to the numbers and not enough to our customers, our service, or even in following leads that we normally would have shared with each other.

"Most of us ended up leaving for the competition. Forrest ended up losing his job. He still blames that third quarter, and us."

A team is only as strong as its attitude, and the attitude is shaped by its leader. If the culture of your department is negative, the results will be the same. Oh, you may be able to function at a cursory level, but just imagine how much more you could achieve if you were to focus on the strengths and successes of your team instead!

Many managers relate too closely to their title, forgetting that you *manage* things but *lead* people. They try too hard to manage every aspect of the work day and they forget that they're actually dealing with human beings who have so much more than just work skills to offer.

While trying to avoid the very humanness of the workplace, these managers fall into the trap of becoming a disciplinarian, a babysitter, or a counsellor – rather than a leader. In trying to control the situation, they only make things worse.

What may be effective treatment for those in prison, daycares, or the military does not translate into the modern working world. Remember, both you and your staff are there by choice.

## You Punish Like a Drill Sergeant

> *You will not be punished for your anger; you will be*
> *punished by your anger.*
> ~ Buddha

Paulette remembers the manager that single-handedly destroyed her once close-knit team of cashiers for a busy department store, "We used to all work together, from trading shifts to grabbing lines for each other when it got busy. We did our best to keep the lines short for each other, especially around the holidays. He found out that two checkers had been hand-entering codes, rather than using the scanners. Even though this didn't affect the bottom line and actually enabled those two to move their lines quicker, since the stupid scanners didn't work half the time, he decided this was a personal insult or something. It's like he went on the warpath because we wouldn't tattle on each other.

"First, he took away all overtime. This left us seriously short-staffed at night, and took away some valuable income for some of us with kids. Then, he knocked our lunch breaks from one hour to half an hour – we barely had time to make it to the back room to clock out before we had to be back on the floor. Finally, he withheld all vacations – even those he had already agreed to – until someone told him who had been doing it.

"The stupid thing is that he knew who it was, all he had to do was look at the logins. I swear, he just wanted us to turn on each other. When the two checkers were finally fired, no one trusted anyone again. It became everyone for themselves, even after he left. Lines got longer and no one cared. We knew we couldn't depend on each other or the company anymore. It didn't matter, though, because it was only a few months after that that our branch was shut down."

A blanket punishment demotivates the entire team, making them afraid of doing anything at all. At best, you will pit them against each other and build resentment while decreasing efficiency and teamwork. It is another passive-aggressive way to shirk your duties as a leader.

## YOU USE RATING SYSTEMS

*One man's transparency is another's humiliation.*
*~ Gerry Adams*

"Jonas felt that it would motivate everyone in the office if he posted our "rating" in the break room," says Kurt. "He gave us each a 1-4 score, which could change from week to week based on our output or his whim or whatever...none of us really knew. We just knew that it sucked. Pretty soon the rumors started as to who was doing what to and for him. Yeah, that helped. We all ended up hating each other only slightly more than we hated Jonas."

It is your job to communicate with individuals on your team where they stand and how they may improve. It is not your job to publically humiliate them.

Public rating systems do not motivate your team. Instead, they condemn your team to unhealthy competition. Rating systems do not create teams, they destroy them.

A public rating system is yet another passive-aggressive way to demotivate and victimize your team. You can certainly do better than that.

## YOU BOW TO THE TATTLETALE

*Gossip is the art of saying nothing in a way that leaves practically nothing unsaid.*
*~ Walter Winchell*

Chelsea had an interesting meeting with her manager at least once a week, "It seemed every other day we were in a conversation that began with, "It has come to my attention," or "Someone has reported..." I felt like I had a five-year-old sister constantly tattling on me for the stupidest things, from not making coffee after finishing the pot to not leaving a sign on my computer screen when I went to the bathroom. Most of it was stuff that had nothing to do with my job, but I got chewed out all the time anyway. I knew who it was, and I wanted to strangle her. Talk about passive-aggressive bullshit. Instead of telling the child-minded little twit to knock it off, my stupid manager perpetuated her tattling."

Each person has different ways of dealing with their frustrations. Some like lots of stage time, while some are much quieter about their issues. This doesn't mean that one is better than the other, so don't pick your favorite and assume their side of the story is the only one.

Tattletales love to waste your time. If you listen to them, they will continue to spend their workday trying to find anything they can to bring back to you. What happens to their productivity then? The more you listen, the more you condone their childish behavior, and the less they (and you) get done.

# ARE YOU A SNIPER OR A LEADER?

*I had several different bosses during the early years of 'Dilbert.' They were all pretty sure I was mocking someone else.*

~ Scott Adams

If you're lucky, you recognized yourself at least in some way in one or more of the above examples. You may have even been given this copy with a particular page dog-eared, bookmarked, or highlighted. Why are you lucky? You are lucky because that recognition is your first step to unlearning those bad habits and replacing them with effective leadership skills.

My hope (and trust me, I share this with your entire team) is that you are simply unaware of your foibles and that you do truly desire to be a healthier, more productive leader. This awareness is the first step. *Desire* to change is the second step.

Don't worry; you won't have to do ten more steps. You only get one more: Gain and use your highly specialized tools. In other words, read on. Learn how to **cultivate**, **motivate**, and **celebrate** your team.

It's not too late. You learned those ineffective skills, you can UN-learn them! In fact, it would be even easier to forget them and learn new ones to replace them - so get cracking. When you put your newfound knowledge into action, you and your team will be unstoppable.

# PART 2: YOUR HIGHLY SPECIALIZED TOOLS

*If you wish to succeed in managing and controlling
others - learn to manage and control yourself.*
~ William Boetcker

Just like the sniper, you have some highly specialized tools at your disposal. Besides his weapon, the most important tool a sniper has is his superior training. As a successful leader, your weapons are more plentiful. They include your ability to **cultivate**, **motivate**, and **celebrate** your team.

CULTIVATING your team means giving it everything it needs to grow healthy and prosper. This involves not only your superior leadership, but the rest of the team's makeup. If you cultivate a supportive, creative, and challenging environment, you will be able to attract and keep the cream of the crop.

MOTIVATING your team goes far beyond simply encouraging them. It does not involve punishing or micromanaging – both of which may show immediate results but destroy your team and your integrity in the long run. Your ability to clearly communicate, appreciate, and delegate tasks, without suffocating your employees, will spin off into unlimited innovation and success.

Money is not the only answer – in fact, it's not even the best motivator! Knowing how each member of your team differs in his or her motivational factors plays a very important part in how you will inspire them to be the best they can be.

CELEBRATING your team's efforts through constructive feedback, meaningful praise, and motivational rewards will encourage loyalty and creativity, not to mention both hard and smart work.

# CULTIVATE

> *A wealthy landowner cannot cultivate and improve*
> *his farm without spreading comfort and well-being*
> *around him. Rich and abundant crops, a numerous*
> *population, and a prosperous countryside are the*
> *rewards for his efforts.*
> ~ Antoine Lavoisier

When you cultivate the ground for a garden, you do all of the preparations to make that ground as inviting as possible to the crop you are about to plant. You rid the soil of weeds and other invasive plants. You till the land to make the soil soft and as rock-free as possible. You remove obstacles that block out the sunlight or disrupt the flow of water. You add nutrients needed for strong, healthy seedlings. You water the soil so that your crop has everything it needs to grow. Then, you plant the healthiest, most diverse seed crops you can find, keeping in mind the types that grow cooperatively.

As grade-schoolers, many of us got to grow bean sprouts in science class. One thing some of us learned is that you can't go digging up the seeds every couple of hours to make sure they're growing – or they will never grow at all. You have to trust that you've prepared the environment with everything they need to grow, and then back off and let them find their way.

When you cultivate your workforce, you are planning to succeed in growing the best team possible. This means you may have to do some weeding so that the environment is healthy. You may have to remove obstacles and add some resources so that your team has everything it needs to function efficiently. You will keep and hire the best and then ensure they have all the tools they need for the job at hand. This includes training, cross-training, and working diligently to keep your best candidates challenged and engaged. Then, back off and watch the magic happen.

## PULLING THE WEEDS

> *Firing is not something you do to someone: firing is something you do for someone.*
> ~ Larry Winget

You understand that you must have a healthy environment so that your dynamic team can grow. But, what do you do with those bad employees?

"Bad" is a big, subjective word that can encompass many things. I've found that most problems arise from lack of communication and direction. A large portion of those "bad" employees are simply reacting to poor leadership. Typically, the troubled employee can be turned around by being treated like an adult, motivated like an asset, and acknowledged as a human being.

A note of caution: If you have been a misguided (or even terrible) boss and are just now trying some of the techniques in this book to turn your style and your team around, give your weeds a chance to adjust. They may just come around when they realize that the culture has shifted and their needs are finally being met. They might not be weeds at all. They might be flowers in that awkward stage right before a growth spurt.

If, however, that person simply will not join you in the campaign to create a better workplace, it may be time to motivate them and your team by letting them go.

How can firing people motivate them? Typically, it won't. You are going to offer this person a choice, and they may choose to be in victim mode. This means they won't learn from their mistake nor be motivated to do better. You can only hope that someday they will take responsibility for their choices.

If you have a problem child that disrupts the workplace, that person can certainly demotivate the rest of your team. If you have tried everything in this book to motivate them and they are not responding, you may just have a weed. It's time to pull them out.

It's rare, but there really are negative, self-serving individuals that will poison the entire structure of your team. Nothing you can do will change them. You can offer increases in pay, accolades, daily donuts, even corner offices and trips to Tahiti and these people will continue to:

- Backstab
- Gossip
- Circumvent
- Tattle
- Manipulate
- Sabotage
- Do as little as possible

Who needs them?

Of course, this might mean actually firing someone. For the first time in your life you can honestly use the line, "It's not you, it's me." Or us, as the case may be. They are a bad fit, and your culture does not work with their type. They're unhappy, you're unhappy. It will be best for all involved to move on. They might even find their calling in the process – perhaps another place where their work style will fit right in.

Some people like to keep to themselves and abhor the idea of working with a team. They will come up with elaborate ways to avoid meetings, events, and anything fun or engaging. Set them free. They'll be happier as long-haul truck drivers.

Some people don't like change and will resist it every step of the way. They'll whine, complain, sabotage progress, and fight training. They feel that things are fine the way they are, no matter how archaic the system. They will hold your entire team back. Don't let them. They can go work for the DMV.

Some people are so focused on the wrongs of others that they enjoy gossiping, ruining their coworker's reputations, and can't wait to tattle if anyone should do something they deem wrong. Send them back to kindergarten where they can try again to grow up and learn some manners. They may want to become politicians or news commentators.

Some people are so cynical that they are totally unwilling or unable to have fun, be creative, or see the good in others. Let them work for the IRS.

Some people show up for the paycheck, and nothing else. You can do nothing to motivate them. They simply don't care. They are drones who will do only the bare minimum to get them from day to day. Once you determine that they cannot be helped out of their chronic depression (which very well could be the issue), let them go. You don't need drifters. They will easily assimilate into a mailroom or grave digging position. No sense in letting them dig your grave.

Now you know who you need to pull. The trick with weeds is that you can't just yank most of them out of the ground because you will shake loose their seeds, which will spread. They will continue to sprout up all around your carefully tended garden. Each weed must be carefully removed and encouraged not to root again nearby. How do you let someone go in the most mutually beneficial way?

Treat them with respect. Set boundaries. Don't let the situation fester. Read on.

## THE MOST BENEVOLENT OUTCOME

Firing someone stinks and is no fun. If you enjoy it, you are in the wrong position. Don't worry, if you *do* enjoy it, there are plenty of prisons that could use your expertise. You might even get your own TV show. Meanwhile, please stop torturing the rest of us and move yourself onto a position better fitting a sadist.

For the rest of us, there are certain steps you must take to both protect yourself and create the most benevolent outcome for all involved. In this case, letting someone go will benefit both the individual and your team. Even if they can't see it immediately, they need to move on.

If there is one word you take away from this section, make it this: DOCUMENT. You cannot have enough documentation. Begin the minute you see an issue. That doesn't mean you've given up on this person, it just means you will be covered should it come to that. It also helps in keeping that person accountable because you will be offering them a clear choice to stay or leave.

Before you do get to that point, provide every opportunity to empower the person first. Often, it is a lack of ownership that leads to disciplinary issues. They have lost the will to care because nothing they do matters. Make it matter – in a good way.

Remember, you are trying to change a dynamic that many are used to, in fact most have grown up with, so there may be some pushback. Ensure that this troubled person has been an ongoing problem and isn't just reacting to change. Firing someone should be an absolute last resort.

Take a deep breath. Remember you're doing this for the good of the team, your sanity, and, ultimately, for the good of the person in question.

Now for the bad news:

You cannot fire someone because of their ATTITUDE.

If you've had endless discussions about this person's attitude, and you've seen no change – or it's gotten worse – it is because the concept of attitude is too personal and too vague. Discussing another person's attitude is combative and judgmental and provides no avenue for growth or change. You are simply saying that you don't like their personality. They typical response to "I don't like your attitude" is "Sucks to be you."

Can you see why it's getting you nowhere?

Many of my workshop participants now ask, "But what if they *do* have an attitude problem, what am I supposed to discuss with them?" Let me ask you this: Can you clearly define what that attitude is in such a way that it can be recreated on paper for those who have neither seen this person in action nor even met them?

If you find yourself listing specific examples of things they've done, not done, or said – you've answered your own question.

Do not discuss attitude. Discuss specific events and behaviors. Now you are asking them to change their behavior, something tangible. You are not asking them to change their attitude, something vague and personal.

This helps you with your documentation, too. If you do not see improvement, you will have specific, universally understood examples of events that clearly paint the picture of this person's behavior. If you do see improvement, you'll know exactly what and when to celebrate!

Now it's time to discuss a particular behavior that needs correction and enlist their help to create a Battle Plan to save their job.

## THE BATTLE PLAN

You hired his person for a reason. If you didn't, your predecessor did. That means someone saw something in this person and felt they'd make a good addition to the team. Assuming their interview skills don't include political-candidate-grade lying, that means there is something worthwhile in this person that, hopefully, can be preserved – if not nurtured. Start there.

To ensure the most benevolent outcome, try everything you can to rediscover the wonderful qualities that got this person hired in the first place. Bring them in and create a Battle Plan to take them to the next level.

Their Battle Plan should include the following:

1. The date and time of the meeting
2. The date of expected execution and completion of the tasks on the Battle Plan (be specific!)
3. Clearly defined behaviors (or performance measures, etc.) that are NOT satisfactory
4. The consequences of continuing those behaviors (yes, including termination)
5. Clearly defined tasks that must be completed, including time span and accuracy/quality of each
6. Clear, measurable goals that must be met to complete those tasks (see S.W.I.F.T. goal setting)
7. The consequences of meeting those goals (yes, rewards!)
8. Any tools, training, or coaching that they may need to achieve the goals or correct the behavior, including how they will be provided and when (be specific!)
9. Signatures – yours and theirs

By creating this Battle Plan, you are showing that you value the individual both as an employee and a person. You are clearly defining the behavior that must stop and the performance required for the position. You are offering incentives to improve and measures so that those improvements will be evident. You are acknowledging if there are any gaps in training, processes, or equipment and offering a fix so it is not a hindrance to performance. You are clearly defining what the consequences are if improvement is not seen. Finally, you are offering them a choice.

It is now up to that person to choose.

## NO IFS, ANDS, OR BUTS

You've documented their behavior. You've created a Battle Plan. You've provided your seedling with every possible tool and avenue for improvement, yet they have chosen not to utilize them.

That's just it. They have made the choice. This is one of those times that the sniper and leader agree – stick to your guns.

You've clearly outlined the consequences of their actions, now follow through. If you were clear in the Battle Plan, they are fully aware of what choice they made. Let them go.

Don't be the jerk that makes them work a full week and fires them on Friday night or Christmas Eve. Don't be passive-aggressive and just stop adding their name to the schedule. You are better than that. The Battle Plan had a date on it. Stick to it. Add a time, if it helps. Just be consistent.

How do you stop the gossip mill on this one? Don't let it get started. If you've been clearly communicating with each member of your team, they know that you go out of your way to ensure each person is aware of their progress and areas that need improvement. They trust that you have given everyone a fair chance and plenty of coaching to work toward a mutually beneficial end. They are a team, after all, and they are aware of the weakest members. They've seen your efforts, and they know that you gave that person a choice. In fact, that person probably broadcasted it any chance they could – those stuck in the victim mentality tend to seek attention like that. If anyone does ask, be honest and let them know that the person in question chose to leave.

Now you and your team can exhale a big sigh of relief.

## FINDING THE RIGHT SEEDS

> *Surround yourself with the best people you can find,*
> *delegate authority, and don't interfere.*
> ~ *Ronald Reagan*

Yes, different people have different talents. They will excel at things that are not mentioned on their resume and often stink at things that are listed. They key is to make your team holistic with different skills, strengths, and styles throughout. The more variety, the better equipped your team will be.

The workplace is more diverse today than ever before. This is a beautiful thing! It means that your team can have a myriad of different insights, ideas, and innovations. It means that you can have people from every generation, gender, and geography. It means that you can have awesome potlucks!

Sure, there may be some culture clashes, but most of these are borne of communication gaps. A dynamic team learns how to trust and communicate – and assume best intentions. These are communications skills you'll continue to hone.

As you hire, seek these differences. Hire people vastly different from one another, and especially different from you.

## WHO TO HIRE. HINT: IT'S NOT YOU

Oh, if only you could hire yourself over and over. Wouldn't that be perfect? You wouldn't have to train them, you'd all get along, no one would argue over what pizza to order, and you'd finally get something done around here.

Really? Think about it a moment...

You have your own set of skills, strengths, and styles that make perfect sense to you and work well for you and hopefully for your position. But you are not an island. If you hired the same person over and over, you would stagnate with that exact set of skills – and no more.

You'd become obsolete.

It's like eating nothing but broth for the rest of your life. Viable. Maybe even tasty, but who wants to live on broth alone? Mix it up! Add some flavor, substance, and variety. Each different component you add to your soup makes it more interesting, nutritious, and delicious.

You have particular skills that benefit the department, and each individual should, as well. If each member has the same skills and personality, you are stuck.

Think of the skills of each member of the old series *Mission: Impossible*. (If you haven't watched them, take a gander – but not the newer movies. They missed the point in the movies.) Each member of the team had specific abilities that enabled every mission to be successful. Sure, many of these skills overlapped – and that's to be expected. It enables them to work better together.

If you are a manager of a bank, you will need math whizzes and tax geniuses and you won't need an electronics specialist, a super model, or a master of disguises...

...or will you?

Each different person you add to your team adds new perspectives, ideas, and talents. Sure, you want to get along with each other. For instance, if you are a busy mailroom that listens to the radio you certainly don't want someone who hates music. Still, wouldn't it be fun to explore different types of music throughout the week?

After you have determined that your pool of candidates have the knowledge and skills for the job opening, hire one of them that is smarter than you. Hire someone of a different generation, color, gender, religion, or political stripe. These people will have fresh ideas, different perspectives, and valuable insights that will enliven your team.

Ultimately, each one of your new hires will contribute to a versatile team that will make *you* look good.

## THIS IS NOT YOUR FAMILY

There are many companies that brag that they treat their employees like "family." Gosh, I hope they're joking. Who is your family? Mine is a hodge-podge mix of neuroses and jealousies and oddness wrapped up in a bunch of people I'd never choose to befriend. I love my family, but I certainly wouldn't want to work with them.

We don't get that choice. We have to put up with them because they're...well...family.

This is not true at the office. Even if you are deep into nepotism, every person on your team is there by *choice*. You or your predecessor *chose* to hire them. They continually *choose* to work there. They can *choose* to leave, and you can *choose* to fire them. This is a relationship much different from family.

If you try to treat your staff like family, you are inviting the same favoritism, tattling, competing, whining, and parenting that exists in every family.

Why do that to yourself?

Treat everyone fairly and professionally. This is not your family. This is a viable, growing, successful business. Or, at least it will be if you see your team as coworkers and not siblings.

## THE MYTH OF THE PURPLE SQUIRREL

Recruiters have long searched for the perfect candidate who has all of the education, skills, and experience to swoop in and excel in a job with no training. They call this elusive creature "The Purple Squirrel."

While it's nice to dream about that perfect candidate, perfection does not exist. If it did, we'd be so bored with it that it would no longer be perfect. The purple squirrel is unrealistic.

In his book, *Purple Squirrel: Stand Out, Land Interviews, and Master the Modern Job Market*, Google recruiter Michael B. Junge tells job seekers how they can make themselves appear to be this special critter and stand out in the ever-growing pool of candidates. It teaches a very specific process to getting the attention that you need so that you can get noticed by companies, interviewed, and, hopefully, hired. This is an art form in appearing to be something you are not.

Meanwhile, in the real world, there have been actual sightings of wild purple squirrels. All have been proven to be fake, in that they somehow ran amok of things such as printer toner or aggressive berries. There are no truly purple squirrels.

Our tendency to strive toward Mr. or Ms. Right in the business world is somewhat like our desire to find Mr. or Ms. Right in our personal lives. We have the preconceived notion of what the perfect person must be – right down to their hairstyle, how they take their coffee, and the type of car they drive. We hold out for that perfect shade of purple and the perfect breed of squirrel and overlook the person who may, very well, be better than perfect.

When recruiting, you have a very specific job description – if not, go back and fix that. Use that and the Dealmaker Exercise to find your candidate. What's right for your team may look drastically different than what you envisioned. Be open to taking that chance.

I'm not saying anyone should settle for Mr. or Ms. "You Might Do." What I am saying is that often we are so focused on our idea of perfection that we miss out on Mr. or Ms. "Right for My Team." There is a significant difference.

## THE WHOLE IS GREATER THAN ITS PARTS

While the diversity and individuality of your team members is very important, keep in mind that a team is not good because of one person's abilities. You may be tempted to hire the superstar – but will that person really benefit the team as a whole?

If you find yourself getting overly excited about a candidate, take a step back. Begin asking those difficult questions:

- Do I want them because they are rock stars or because they will round out my team?
- Are they special because they possess skills our team is lacking, or are they just seriously awesome on paper?
- Are they teachable?
- Are they able to share their knowledge with the rest of the team?
- Are they even a team player?
- Will they not only fit into, but enjoy, our team culture?

You are building an incredible team. There will be growing pains. But, and this is very important, whenever hiring a new person ask: 'Am I growing my team or just expanding it?'

## THE DEALMAKER EXERCISE

This is a simple exercise that will clarify for you what you're looking for in a candidate. If you are honest with yourself and willing to spend some time at the front end, you will save a lot of time and frustration on the back end.

Fold a piece of paper into thirds (as if you were going to mail a letter). Label each section as follows:

For this exercise, you are focusing on the deal makers, not the deal breakers. You know quite clearly what the deal breakers are, whether it's smoking, sarcastic wit, dog haters – whatever. Why focus on the negative? You will only be inviting more of that in. Instead, you will focus only on the positive aspects of the candidate you are searching for.

Under "Absolutely must have," list all of the hard skills that the candidate must have in order to do the job. These are non-negotiable and must be at the top of the job description when you post it. These skills should be listed on their resume or somewhere in their cover letter. You won't waste your time with interviewing those that don't at least have these skills.

Under "Can learn," list any skills – hard or soft – that a person can learn on the job. These are things that they may have had some related experience in, they are somewhat knowledgeable about, or that you are pretty sure they would be able to pick up. You'll recognize whether they are teachable when using some of the interview techniques outlined in the next chapter.

Be very honest here. Revisit your "Absolutely must haves" and see if any of those can be moved over to "Can learn." You do not want to miss out on your best and brightest candidates because you are inflexible on super-specific skills. Can they be learned on the fly or honed on the job? For instance, if you need someone who makes a mean pivot table, a candidate that is an advanced Excel user may not have ever needed to use pivot tables, but will be able to learn rather quickly. A good candidate will have learned by the second interview, if you ask them to.

Under "Nice to have," list all of those extras that aren't required for the job but would benefit the team in other ways. Have fun with this – list a few things like bakes cookies, plays basketball or bowls (if you have a company team or league), or can fix a copier. These won't help you decide who to interview, but they will help you decide between two or three candidates if everything is else is equal.

Do not skip this section! This also gives you some insight into the person as a whole when you are interviewing. When you learn a little bit about their interests, not only does it give you something to talk about that will break the ice, but it will give you insight into their passions and background that will spill over into their work.

As you get to know a candidate, you may add to this column something they mentioned that you hadn't thought of. It's OK to add some extra "Nice to haves" as you go along. It will only clarify the best candidate later.

## WRITE A CLEAR AND FAIR JOB DESCRIPTION

Once you have done the Dealmaker Exercise, it's time to revisit that dusty, old job description. If you wrote one. Many don't, then wonder why they aren't getting what they need out of their employees. If it's missing or generic, write one now.

The clearer, more concise your job description, the better the candidates will be and the less issues you will have after they are hired. A well-written job description protects both you and your employees. Do not think you are saving time by ignoring this or copying a typical description from the internet based loosely on the job title.

Carefully read the job description you have. Does it include specifics, such as the maximum a candidate must be able to lift? Don't kid yourself – files can be heavy! Does it specify how long they will typically have to sit? How much they will have to type? English, grammar, math skills? Don't laugh, these are often overlooked and then regretted later.

Be specific about the duties. If you have a phrase similar to "Other duties as necessary," REMOVE IT! This is a copout. It does not protect you or your employee in any way. It does not hold up in court. It only sets you both up for a "Gotcha!" later. Honestly, this could mean anything from painting the bathrooms to washing your personal car to cat sitting – it means absolutely nothing. A wise candidate would ask you to clarify and then demand it in writing before accepting the position.

If you've already hired those that didn't ask or demand it in writing, look at what you ended up with. Don't you wish you had wiser employees?

If working weekends and overtime is a possibility, list it. Do your best to give a percentage, based on past needs. Overestimate. They won't be upset if the reality turns out to be fewer days or hours over the norm.

Specify the actual working hours, when you expect them to be at their station (not at the time clock, if you use one, but actually on the job). Specify what holidays are given off – paid or unpaid. Be very clear. Specify what holidays you will work. Do not assume they'll do the math based on what you omit. Make it clear.

Specify breaks, lunch hours, and time for training. Be clear about late policies, vacation, and sick leave.

Specify the access they will be allowed to things like the internet, outside resources, training, and even you. These are common deal breakers for candidates – best they are aware of them before applying. You don't want to waste valuable time with people that will be unhappy because they can't pop onto the internet to check the weather report, learn new things about the accounting systems, or brush up on their coding language. They will be glad they were informed beforehand that you are one of those types of bosses that don't trust them with things like internet access or flex time. Your cultures are quite different and simply wouldn't work well together.

You are a valuable resource, too. Candidates want to know if they would not be able to ask you a question or set up a meeting because you're travelling 95% of the time. Some people love autonomy, others wither and die without frequent instruction. Best to have this right in the job description so both sides know what they're getting into.

Job orientation training is way too late to learn about these things. This is like finding out that your new spouse hates your favorite pet, is allergic to your favorite food, and won't stand to listen to your favorite music – all the day AFTER the honeymoon! You've made a commitment, so you'll stay in the relationship...until you die inside. Then, it's on to someone who will be more honest up front. Yes, you've done this to your employees! That's why you're looking for new ones.

Make your job description as detailed and clear as possible so that you can eliminate excuses – from both sides – as to who is responsible for what, when, and why.

## INTERVIEWS THAT DON'T STUMP, SPANK, OR STINK

> *A company should limit its growth based on its ability*
> *to attract enough of the right people.*
> *~ Jim Collins*

During the interview process, the types of questions you ask will have a definite effect on the type of people you will end up hiring. What you are looking for is to reveal the true individual. This is the person you will eventually see after you hire them, so it's best to get it out in the open now. Spending the extra time on this side of the hiring process will save you days – if not weeks – of heartache and hassle on the other side, not to mention productivity and the possibility of lawsuits.

Remember, it's a two-way street: They are interviewing you, too. How you set the tone now affects how they perceive the job, should they accept it, the company they'll become part of, and whether they are going to fit in or will even bother trying.

Yes, some people will accept a job without fully understanding what the company's culture or expectations are. Some, simply because they need the money. Why open yourself up to that? Do your homework and ask better questions.

### AVOID REHEARSED ANSWERS

The old, "Where do you see yourself in five years?" is an impractical, outdated question that no one will answer honestly if they are sane. First of all, it's a no-win question: Either you will find them too ambitious ("I see myself in your position.") or too unambitious ("I don't know. It depends on what happens here.") If they have an answer at the ready, it's a *rehearsed* answer, meaning it's useless. You aren't interviewing the person to find out how well they prepared mini speeches. You want to find out what makes that person tick and whether they'd be a good fit for your organization.

Flat-out ask them what excites them about this position. Hopefully it's more than money.

Instead of asking them about their greatest strengths (being able to lie under pressure) and weaknesses (it's always perfectionism or that they are workaholics), ask them about a specific incident and how it affected others, such as missing a deadline or dropping the ball. Ask them what they did to correct it, and what they learned. Now you've got some honesty, hopefully a little empathy toward those they failed, and a deep look at their integrity and problem-solving abilities.

If they try to sell you on having never failed, you certainly don't want them on your team. First of all, because it's a lie. Second, because you can only learn from failure. You want someone who is human and can learn.

Ask what motivates and frustrates them. Ask what management style they prefer. You can rule yourself out by the answers to these questions, especially if they are thoughtful and you are the opposite of what would help them flourish. This is where you'll have to be honest with yourself.

## PLAY FAIR

Stop asking about the job they currently hold or recently left. The job they're applying for is probably quite similar. Instead, go back a ways. Ask them about their first job and why they took it (motivation). Ask them about the job that taught them the most (gratitude and teachability). Ask them what about that job they found wasn't a good fit and what they did about it (accountability).

Stop asking them what they made at their last position. This is a trap, and it's unfair. They are aware of what you are willing to pay. If not, then you have failed to write a clear job description. (What's the holdout? Are you afraid people will only apply for the money? Trust me, no one pays that well.) You've already sorted out the folks without the baseline skills and experience you're looking for, so the playing field is relatively level. Their past income has no bearing on the new arrangement. That's like asking a first date how much their last date made or whether they were better looking. Why are you comparing yourself to something that is no longer in play?

If you are using this question to determine how much you'll offer them, you are being dishonest. Do you truly believe they will be honest in return? What is their motivation? You have begun the relationship with game playing. Now they know what to expect from you once hired.

## DO YOUR HOMEWORK

Speaking of dating, stop saying, "Tell me about yourself." It's too open-ended and expects narcissism from folks that might not fit that mold. It's a rude question when you're dating and ruder still when you're interviewing. Say what you mean. Be more specific. Try questions like, "What first interested you in accounting?" or "How did you go from a zoology degree to database administration?" It shows that you did *your* homework, too. It confirms that you actually read all of that paperwork you made them fill out and that you actually have an interest in them. It illustrates how you will treat them, should you hire them. Conversely, they'll feel appreciated and want to know more about your company.

## CHECK THEIR HOMEWORK

You want to see if they've done their homework, too. Ask them how they will contribute to the company's mission. Ask them about the value statement, if it is easily accessible, and how it aligns with their personal values. A truly interested candidate will have looked both of these up – or at least read them in the lobby while waiting for you to meet with them.

You have deal-breakers, ask them what theirs are. This is a really good indicator of whether they fully read the job description, and/or whether you wrote it well. Sometimes, you might get some pretty pointed questions or comments that will really shine a light on their mindset – things like, "Would I really have to work weekends?" or "I am hoping that, eventually, I'd be able to work from home." It may come out as a casual comment – but be wary. These preset ideas can make or break their motivation later on.

Ask them what the top three things they'd do in their new position if they had free reign. Look for creativity, strategy, prioritization skills, and risk-taking. This is a ballsy question to ask and answer. It will also show you if they have done any research on the industry, if not your company, specifically.

## BE SPECIFIC

Instead of finishing the interview by asking, "Do you have any questions for me?" (SNORE!), ask something more specific, such as, "Now that you know a bit more about the position, what skills are you excited to bring or add to our team?" or "What sort of guidance or mentorship are you interested in either providing or pursuing?"

The important thing to note here is that you are asking open-ended questions. Asking a question that can be answered with

"Yes" or "No" doesn't help you learn a thing about the person in front of you. Ask questions that get them talking!

## MODEL RESPECT

This may seem elementary, but be on time to the interview. Nothing says "corporate jerk" like making a candidate wait well past the set time for an interview. If you set that in motion, they will not understand why you hold them to different standards and expect them to be on time to work. Remember, you are their first impression and example.

If you are not getting the types of candidates you are looking for, it may very well be because there is word on the street about your hiring practices. If you're disrespectful, ask inane questions, don't follow up, or are generally dismissive, folks will warn each other off. If you are those things in a first impression, imagine how awful it would be to work with you day after day? Yes, you are being judged by these things, as well you should.

## FOLLOW UP!!!

Let everyone you interview know, every step of the way, what the next step will be and whether they will be part of it. Your respectful actions throughout this process will keep the doors open should you need to revisit the pool of qualified candidates again. If you interviewed someone who was in college and the schedules didn't work out, imagine missing out on them after they graduate because you were simply too rude to shoot them a short email or letter letting them know that they didn't make the cut.

No news is never good news. In fact, it's obnoxious.

Hopefully, if you've learned anything so far, you've learned that it's not all about you. If you want the best candidates, you will have to be the best employer – and this means beefing up your interview skills. Viable candidates are not numbers. They are not to be used. Treat people with the respect they deserve, and it will come back to you on and off the job.

Now you've built the ultimate team – let's keep the players!

## KEEPING THE CREAM OF THE CROP

> *I am convinced that nothing we do is more important*
> *than hiring and developing people. At the end of the*
> *day you bet on people, not on strategies.*
> *~ Larry Bossidy*

It takes a lot to make a relationship work, and – make no mistake
– you have a relationship with each of your teammates. Honestly,
with whom do you spend the most time? Eight to twelve hours a
day, five to six days a week – it's your team at work.*

If you have been fortunate enough to build or inherit an
incredible team of amazing people, you'll want to do anything
that isn't illegal or immoral to keep them. This means you'll have
to offer some crystal-clear goals, increase the feeling of fulfillment
of their role within the team, and offer some kick-ass training and
incentives. Start by finding out what they want to grow into, then
set some clear objectives and motivating goals.

*By the way, if you are spending more than 40 hours a week at
your job, visit the idea of delegating.*

## CHALLENGE THEM

*There is nothing like a challenge to bring out the best
in man.*
~ *Sean Connery*

We'll talk more about motivating your team in the next section, but this bears a special mention. Your *best* performers need development, too! You will lose as many good people to boredom as you will to poor leadership. Your top performers are at the top of their game because they enjoy the challenge. Offer them more.

This may mean more training. This may mean diverse training. It may mean a mentorship – where they are either the mentor or the mentored. It may very well mean giving them more to do or coaching them toward a management position – even yours.

Be careful not to get complacent and ignore your highest achievers, or you might lose them. Cultivating the best will only make you look better.

Be honest with them. Remember to give them feedback and ask them what interests them and what they're looking forward to or what you can do to make their jobs more challenging, engaging, or exciting. Then, let them speak. Don't offer suggestions – see what makes them tick first!

# TRAIN

> *Learning without thought is labor lost; thought without learning is perilous.*
> ~ *Confucius*

It's amazing how often training is treated as a luxury or something that isn't worth the time, particularly because so much time will be saved if you and your team are properly trained! The only way you will have a productive team is if every member is fully and appropriately trained.

This does not mean just technical skills, either. You are no longer able to come in with pure, hard skills and function at any level of competence without the ability to interact with the diverse workforce around you. It is shortsighted to believe that hard skills, alone, will fulfill the duties of yours or any position.

The more training and opportunity for training that you offer, the more your employees will know that you are willing to invest in them. They will be more valuable to the team and the company's mission.

Training not only increases competence, it creates loyalty and surges creativity. The more you learn, the more you'll want to learn.

## TRAIN YOU

A sniper will use his specialized training not only to do his job well, but to get himself out of a sticky situation when things go awry. Bear in mind that he doesn't just train once and is considered "trained up" for life. He goes back for refreshers and updates on new technology and techniques – and he practices. Constantly. He always knows what he is and what his job expectations are. Do you?

Anyone can learn the skills involved with being a competent sniper, but, obviously, it takes a special type of person to actually *want* to be one.

Are you a true leader? It's OK to admit it if you're not. Not everyone *wants* to be a leader. If you are a boss but not a true leader, you only have a title and no purpose. You aren't helping anyone – your team or yourself. So, reassess.

Anyone can learn the skills to be a good leader, but it takes a special type of person who actually *wants* to be a leader. There is absolutely no shame in in not wanting to be a leader – unless you slap yourself into the role for the money or because you felt forced into it and hang on for the sake of hanging on.

Do you find joy in leading? Be honest! Where do you find the most joy?

Money is not your only motivator. If it is, then you are not a true leader. This answers your question right away. Perhaps your career path is not one that involves leadership so much as return on investments. Have you considered being an entrepreneur or a broker? If you are good at sales and motivated by profit, then think about taking a role that does not involve you leading a team. You will find that you're happier and more successful if you play to your strengths.

If you have other motivators – particularly the desire to serve others (yes, good leaders serve), then you may indeed be a candidate for leadership. You may only need some decent training. The fantastic news is that anyone can learn leadership skills. You only need the desire.

Successful people never stop learning. Leadership training is plentiful, and it is effective – but only if you participate fully. Education is not a one-time affair, it is a continual process. You will want to improve yourself in many ways, such as taking classes, attending workshops, reading books like this one, going to leadership retreats and events – anything that boosts your talents and diminishes your weak areas. Even if you take the same class or read the same book several times, you will learn something new each time. You are a different person than you were the first time you took that class or read that book, so you will get something different. Plus, you may have forgotten more than you learned after a while – refreshers rock!

Keep a personal library of resources so that you can refer back to them as often as you like. If you are struggling with a concept or situation, you may already have the answer at hand.

Meanwhile, practice. Learn from your mistakes. Hone your skills. Listen to feedback. Refine again.

You should not only be proficient in leadership and communication skills, but in the technical aspects of the team you are leading. If you don't understand the job that each member of your team does, how can you lead them? How can you encourage them to become better? You don't have to be better than they are at it – just understand it enough that you can answer questions or lead them in the right direction. Better yet, understand it enough that you can step in and do it, at least at the base level, when they need help or are not present.

## TRAIN THEM

While you're at it, take potential new leaders with you. As you learn how to more effectively cultivate, motivate, and celebrate your team, you'll find that the more you share information, the more powerful the results. Invest in your team. When you find a program or some materials that really help you, offer the same to them. The more you share, the further you will go together.

At the very least, allow your team to seek learning opportunities whenever they desire. This can be through formal means, workshops, even mentorships. Your willingness to invest in them this way will create loyalty and job ownership that not only empowers the individual but strengthens the team as a whole.

As new hires, each person should be armed with a clear, precise job description. From that, they will be able to determine what training or refreshers they might need to hit the ground running.

The more comprehensive the training, the faster they will become productive members of the team and the faster their confidence will build, meaning more accuracy and innovation.

Each position should have SOPs (Standard Operating Procedures) that clearly explain, step by step, the essential elements of each task. It does not have to be so precise that there is no room for improvement or invention – allow your employees to own their positions by allowing them to do it their way. You explain what and why. You only need to coach them in the how, as needed.

How do you come up with SOPs for each position on your team? Ask each member to create them! These should be living documents, shared with all members. As a new person fills the role, ask them to update the SOPs as they learn more or their position grows.

Each member of your team should not only know where the collection of SOPs lies, but be encouraged to read and update positions other than their own. That way, should someone go on vacation or leave suddenly, the rest of the team can jump in and take over. This will help immensely with cross-training.

If any of your team lacks technical skills, bring them up to speed. It can be very demoralizing to get behind because you simply do not understand how to do your job. You know they are teachable, so let them learn! Ask them to bring back their newfound knowledge and share with the team any tricks or tips or new ideas.

## CROSS-TRAIN

> *Individuals, too, who cultivate a variety of skills seem*
> *brighter, more energetic, and more adaptable than*
> *those who know how to do one thing only.*
> *~ Robert Shea*

Imagine a football, baseball, or soccer team where each player only knows his position, but nothing about any of the other players'. No one would know who they are covering, where they are supposed to be, or which way to send the ball. It would be ineffective, and they would continually lose games. Sounds crazy! Yet, we expect this exact scenario in our work teams. Each person has their own little job and their own little area, and no one knows what the others do. How many games have you lost lately?

Cross-training is a vital step in teamwork.

This does not mean that everyone must be an expert at everything. Remember, you want different skills, strengths, and styles throughout your team. Cross-training means you and your team should all know at least a little bit about each other's jobs. In a perfect world, you should all be able to seamlessly fill in for someone who is ill or on vacation. At the very least, you should be able to hold the fort with a skeleton crew.

Cross-training, if done right, can be empowering. You can use it as a way to set up or bolster mentorships and partnerships. It can be a fun way to break up the doldrums of a work week. For instance, set aside an hour or two for the IT guy to hang out with the accountant or the driver to hang out with the packer to see how their jobs affect one another. You will find alliances forming and more efficient and thoughtful processes evolving.

Keep those SOPs updated! When cross-training, you may find some gaps or generalities that need correcting. Allow these new alliances to own their job now and make their position easier for someone new to understand. You'll find that new hires are thrilled with the documentation.

# MOTIVATE

*Have a vision. It is the ability to see the invisible. If you can see the invisible, you can achieve the impossible.*
*~ Shiv Khera*

Motivating your team to do its best and keep on striving for more – even through difficult times – is the essence of your job title. It is so much more than just being an enthusiastic leader.

You will find that motivation flowing as you learn to COMMUNICATE more clearly and effectively. You communicate through so much more than your words. Your character, the way you discipline and reward your team, and how you set and achieve goals are all substantial ways you may not realize are motivating or demotivating your team.

Enjoy getting to know the different personality types, communication styles, and ways to motivate – without money – the individuals on your team. Show that you APPRECIATE them by listening to them and treating them with respect. Create a culture of fun as you add unique traditions that fit your team's personality.

There is no reason for you to be overworked. You have a team to help you accomplish everything you need done, so DELEGATE and get it done! Holding on to work or trying to do it all yourself is an emotionally immature reaction to trust issues. People want to be trusted with challenging projects, and they want to be part of something bigger. Learning how to entrust different projects to a diverse mixture of people shows that you chose wisely and are worthy of following.

Many studies have shown that the number one complaint of unhappy employees is micromanagers. DO NOT SUFFOCATE your team. You worked hard to hire the right people. Back off and let them do what they do best.

## COMMUNICATE

> *Good leaders must communicate vision clearly,*
> *creatively, and continually. However, the vision*
> *doesn't come alive until the leader models it.*
> ~ *John C. Maxwell*

Communicating does not just mean saying something well. It means ensuring understanding – from both sides. Learning to communicate well is the most important thing you can do for your team, your career, and even your home life. What does that mean?

First of all, you have to be clear. If you are not getting the results you want, you are not making yourself clear in the first place. People want to do well. It is human nature to desire to feel productive and appreciated. If you are exceptionally clear on what that looks like, you'll find your team striving to achieve that. If you are not clear, they will strive for what they think that might be – and often miss the mark.

Your job as a leader is not to constantly reprimand and punish your team. Your job is to be a strong enough communicator so that you don't have to. People want to be led by someone they can trust and who they know believes in them. This means that you are in the business of communication more than anything.

The most resounding communication you will ever present is your example.

## YES, CHARACTER MATTERS

> *Live in such a way that you would not be ashamed to*
> *sell your parrot to the town gossip.*
> ~ Will Rogers

As I pointed out earlier, regardless of what the Press says, character does, indeed, matter. You must model the behavior you want to see. This means show up – on time – and work while you're there. Don't lie. Mean what you say. Take the same time for lunches – yes, even if you are salary or exempt. If you have to take more time, inform your team. Allow them the same flexibility you enjoy. If you can't, then don't allow yourself that flexibility. Double standards garner resentment. If you don't believe that, ask a child how he feels about his bedtime being different from his parents' or his older siblings'.

Do these sound like pretty basic principles? I should hope so! But so many "leaders" think that it's OK to live by different standards, you begin to wonder. If you are trying to lead, you've got to walk ahead, but you've got to walk ahead on the same path as your followers.

Your character communicates more than anything you can speak, draw, or imagine. You can preach until you're blue in the face, but if your actions don't follow, you aren't leading.

Once your attitude and actions are exemplary, your feedback will have more weight. For your team to be effective, you must also provide specific feedback early and often.

# THE PUPPY PRINCIPLE

*People - and dogs - are dying to be trained.*
~ *Ian Dunbar*

Before you get into this, please understand that I am not comparing you or anyone on your team to dogs. I am simply saying that the way we condition dogs (and even cats) to trust us and engage in desired behavior directly translates to how we should discipline human beings.

I've trained many amazing dogs throughout the years. I'm often asked how I get my dogs to listen so well and do so many great little tricks. Even the difficult breeds respond to these methods. In human trials, many behavioral scientists have arrived at the same conclusions; though they call it different things: Positive Reinforcement, Operant Conditioning, the list goes on. The principle is that you offer an abundance of positive feedback when the subject is producing the desired results, rather than punishing them for not producing.

Many people balk at this idea because they are afraid that people will only be motivated by rewards. Honestly, this has nothing to do with rewarding! If I trained every animal by offering tasty treats for everything they did, I'd have a lot of fat animals that only responded when food was present. Rewarding is not motivating. It's actually quite backwards to think that offering a reward will motivate someone – because it misses the point of the most basic desires of all creatures.

That being said, dogs, cats, and people are most motivated by two basic things:

1. Food
2. Attention

Food is an easy, cheap, and quick way to motivate pretty much anything. My marketing friend, Lee Kaplanian, says, "Money talks, but chocolate *sings*." It's true, but this fits more under appreciating, which we'll talk about in a bit. For now, let's focus on what really creates long-lasting motivation: Attention.

## THE ATTENTION SPECTRUM

*Negative feedback is better that none. I would rather
have a man hate me than overlook me. As long as he
hates me I make a difference.*

*~ Hugh Prather*

Humans and animals all seek positive attention from their leaders and their peers. Barring this, they will move to any type of attention they can get – even negative – because nothing is worse than no attention at all. The attention spectrum looks like this:

### POSITIVE——NEGATIVE——NONE

Positive attention comes in many forms, and each person will be motivated by a different type of attention (we'll go over those types under Appreciate). The type of attention we're focusing on here is feedback. You'll be hearing this a lot: Feedback should be delivered *early* and *often*.

What does this have to do with puppies? Let's walk through the most basic puppy training. If you've ever raised a dog, then you're familiar with the number-one thing that every puppy must learn:

Housetraining.

How do people traditionally train their dogs? They come home, find the mess, tell the dog he's a bad dog, some rub the dog's nose in it and spank the dog. Then, as the dog sulks, you clean up the mess, continuing to admonish the critter as you do the paper-towel-spot-clean-up-dance. The next day it starts over again. This can take weeks until finally the dog seems to "get" it and stops going in the house. Some dogs are just untrainable and must either become outdoor-only dogs or be sent to the shelter to become someone else's problem.

I have housetrained even the most stubborn dogs in fewer than 8 days.

Understanding the Attention Spectrum, the easy way to motivate a dog is the same principle you can use to motivate people:

- Downplay (or ignore) the bad.
- Present the desired alternative.
- Praise the good.

## DOWNPLAY THE BAD

This is not to say that you must sweep terrible behavior under the rug. If someone is a bully (sexual harassment, threatening physical violence, etc.), this cannot be ignored, it must be addressed immediately. What this part of the principle demonstrates is that simple, annoying, attention-begging behaviors can be eliminated if they are ignored. They are seeking negative attention because they aren't getting the positive attention they so desperately crave. Remember, negative attention is better than no attention.

Imagine you are in a grocery store near a small child who is throwing a temper tantrum. What does that child want? Yes, she's probably screaming that she wants the toy or the candy bar, but what she's really after is attention. Any kind of attention.

If positive attention is not available, our drive to be seen and heard will lead us to seek whatever kind of attention we can get. The louder we are, the more people will pay attention to us. We will do whatever it takes, even seek negative attention. It is certainly better than no attention at all.

There are many ways to be "loud" that do not require screaming and thrashing about on the floor. Passive-aggressive behavior ("I don't get mad, I get even."), crying victimhood, chronic lateness, tattletelling, the list goes on. These are all ways that people seek attention – and by giving it to them, you are motivating them to do it more.

Instead, turn your back on bad behavior. Clean up the puddle and ignore the puppy as you do it. This hurts more than any amount of whacking on the nose with a newspaper.

This even works with cats. (And so many people believe that cats couldn't be trained – ha!)

Imagine having a kitten. She is so cute and fluffy, you love holding her in your arm and playing with her fuzzy little belly. Her sweet, soft paws bop your hands gently.

Until a week later, when the claws come out.

Now every time you play with your kitten, you end up with shredded, bloody hands. What have you done? How do you get kitty to understand that paws are good, claws are bad?

Go back to the universal motivator: Attention. When kitty claws you, stop playing. Take your hand away. Turn your back if you can. After a few times, she will associate the retraction of attention with the bearing of her claws, and she'll stop. What she wants most of all is that attention! When she plays nice, you continue with the attention. Simple, but effective.

In fact, it's so effective that your pets train YOU the same way. The next time you rub kitty's fur the wrong way and she simply gets up and leaves, remember the attention spectrum.

That is why time-outs, if done properly, work so well with children. The child faces the corner, yelling "Can I get out now" or rabid-firing questions. If you respond, you are giving that child what he wants most of all: Attention. You are reinforcing his bad behavior. If you ignore him, however, the timeout becomes more effective. Next time, he'll understand that bad behavior gets him nothing – so why do it? Meanwhile, good behavior gets him what he wants most of all, your attention and his freedom.

## WHY PUNISHMENT BACKFIRES

It may seem frustrating to have to utilize so much patience to recondition someone's behavior when you could simply get immediate results via punishment. Just threaten someone with demotion or termination and they'll shape right up – no fluffy people-skills needed!

Perhaps for a while. A brief, tense, unproductive while.

Punishment does not teach nor help develop good behavior. It only teaches what bad behavior is and encourages the subject not to engage in it – or, at least, to not get caught engaging in it. Fear of punishment merely suppresses the overt practice of the negative behavior – it does not encourage stopping it. In fact, it may inspire your employees to find more creative ways to get away with it.

Do you ever drive over the speed limit? Not bother with your seatbelt? Engage in other "illegal" activities such as purchasing 13 items in the express lane? The threat of punishment does not spur you on to better behavior – it only surges your creativity to find ways to not get caught.

Punishment creates an environment of avoidance. You will completely destroy all lines of communication by engaging in fear tactics. If you want honesty in return, forget it.

Consistent threats and punishment will shut down the subject. The person will simply quit trying to do anything. Why bother? No good will come of doing better or worse.

People and dogs will develop a complex if all they hear is "no" or that they are bad. They will get to the point that they're afraid to do anything at all. They will enter a state of learned helplessness, which makes you and your team useless.

You most likely have felt this way at some point in your life. Be it with a spouse, an organization, a volunteer endeavor, or your parents, you were told you were wrong so many times that at some point you threw your hands up and said something like, "Fine, since I can't do anything right, I'll just stop doing anything at all."

A punitive environment creates backstabbing, tattling, and other negative behaviors that attempt to detract attention from oneself.

Punishment often leads to retaliatory behaviors. If you've been sniped by a subordinate, this is probably why. They got sick of your treatment and went to your superior in effort to get you in trouble, for a change. In dogs, you'll find temporary submissiveness until they attack the punisher. It's the same thing.

Punishment in front of peers multiplies these results.

As you can see, negative reinforcement is simply and only that: negative. Instead, show them what you actually *want* to see in a way that they'll want to see it, too.

## PRESENT THE ALTERNATIVE

Criticizing without building a solution is counter-productive because it creates helplessness in the victim. And, trust me, if you are criticizing someone with no solutions in sight, you are victimizing them. How effective are victims on your team? Not very.

So, build a solution. Offer what can be done differently the next time. Point them toward the desired result. That's the difference between constructive and not. Constructive, meaning building up. Get it?

We'll go into more detail about constructive feedback in a bit.

Back to the puppy: You've ignored the puppy as you cleaned the puddle. Now, take him outside and show him where you WANT him to go. If he does it, even accidentally, tell him what a good dog he is. Continue to praise him whenever he goes where you want him to go.

## PRAISE THE GOOD

Soon, the puppy will be heading out on his own and looking to you for praise, as if to say, "This is what you want, right?" He doesn't need a treat, he just needs reinforcement that he's doing the right thing. Give it to him. After a while, it will be part of his nature and he won't need the constant reinforcement. That is your ultimate goal.

What is important to note is this: feedback must be **early** and **often**. It must be **relevant** and **specific**, too.

When you punish a puppy after the fact, he has positively no idea why he is being punished. It's too late. It has no bearing on his reality now. Sure, he will react with a guilty face, he may even hide as if he knows – but he doesn't. He's only reacting to your anger and not associating his bad behavior with it at all. If you don't believe me, try tossing a paper towel on the ground in front of your adult dog you trained this way. Even if he's done nothing wrong, he'll shrink away from it. He doesn't associate his actions with your anger. He only associates your anger with his being in trouble, and now he associates paper towels with your anger.

The 'woulda coulda shoulda' mentality is disheartening and ineffective. By the time you get to "You should have done _____." It's too late. Wouldn't you want to smash a GPS that said things like, "Oh, you should have turned there..."? Too little too late, and now you're lost.

Instead, offer a way to improve for the next time – you can only control the present. Then, when they do succeed, reinforce that behavior by letting them know that you saw an improvement and they are on the right course.

What about the mess they may have made the first time? This is where people can be better than puppies. Empower them. After explaining what the desired outcome looks like and how to achieve that, ask them for ideas on how to clean up the mess at hand. If they simply don't know, you can coach them through the process. Coach them – don't do it for them! This is a learning moment. We'll talk more about this in Clear Repercussions.

## CREATE A CLEAR MISSION

> *A small body of determined spirits fired by an*
> *unquenchable faith in their mission can alter the*
> *course of history.*
> ~ *Mahatma Gandhi*

If there is one complaint that was universal in all my research, it was that the manager was never clear on what the ultimate goal should be. Every organization must have a mission statement, it means everything in what and how they plan every task. Your department should have a mission statement, too.

If you do not have a mission statement for your department, this is a wonderful opportunity to involve your team. It is an excellent way to clean the slate and reposition yourself and your team as a stronger asset for the organization.

Make your mission clear and concise and everyone will be working with the same values and with an idea of their greater purpose. It will strengthen your team and promote productivity.

When developing your mission with your team, ask them to answer these questions:

- Who are we?
- What do we actually do? Why?
- What do we stand for?
- How do we benefit the organization?
- How do we benefit our ultimate customers? (These can be internal or external)
- How do we benefit each other as a team?

First, brainstorm on these questions. There are no wrong answers, even if some on your team are being smartasses. Give them equal attention. Eventually they will see that you are, indeed, serious and you are willing to invest in them. They'll start to own it and better ideas will flow.

Next, start to narrow down the suggestions to ones that really reflect what your team is – or it wants to be. You'll start to find a pattern.

Now you may begin with the rough drafts. The first one will undoubtedly be long-winded and a little fluffy. Don't worry, you'll be honing, editing, and molding. A lot.

Inc. Magazine says that mission statements should include four key elements: Value, inspiration, plausibility, and specificity. Ensure you're hitting these. Make sure that your mission fits within the organization's mission.

Finally, get it down to a one-sentence mission that is short, sweet, and to the point. Make it something that incites pride throughout your team. Imagine you are a candidate for hire: Would you be excited about the prospect of working with a team with this mission? If yes, you've got it!

By the way, here is a quick and easy way to see if you're on the right track. If your statement sounds like anything generated by the Laughing Buddha Mission Statement Generator (laughing-buddha.net/toys/mission) – reassess. You want ownership and pride, not platitudes and not generalities.

## CLEAR OBJECTIVES

> *The more we elaborate our means of communication,*
> *the less we communicate.*
> ~ *J. B. Priestley*

It may seem obvious, but you simply cannot achieve a goal if you don't know what it is. There is nothing more demotivating than not knowing what your objectives are. If any member of your team doesn't have a clear idea of your direction, of their role in that goal, and of their specific duties, then your leadership is at stake. Your team needs clear direction to function proficiently.

Ensuring you have clearly communicated the objectives requires three steps:

### STEP ONE: SPEAK THE SAME LANGUAGE

I do a listening exercise that involves folding paper with your eyes closed. A pretty simple idea, such as "fold lengthwise" often incites arguments. One person's idea of folding lengthwise is not universal – and no amount of arguing or dictionary-thumping is going to convince someone who holds true the opposite idea. How do you get around something like that and move on?

Create new terms.

When clarifying your team's objectives, you may have to either define or refine some misunderstood terms. Sometimes, it may be best to create new terms altogether.

One of my teams came up with a brilliant way to get rid of the lengthwise argument: Hamburger vs. Hotdog. The paper they were working with was standard-size, so when folded one way, it ended up short and squarish, like a hamburger. Folded the other way, it was long and skinny like a hotdog.

They laughed, they had fun, and they got closer than any other team to meeting the ultimate goal.

The more obvious, outlandish, and/or silly the new terms, the better. They will add to your team's culture and be more memorable. Invite your team members to come up with these ideas. They will enjoy that you are willing to invest in them and listen to them.

Once you are sure you are speaking the same language, you can then engage in two-way feedback that will lead to full understanding. To seek effective communication is not an event, it is an ongoing process.

## STEP TWO: SEEK UNDERSTANDING

When you believe you are on the same page, it is time to employ the secret weapon of clear communication: Listening. Ask the person to translate what they heard, then shut up and let them talk.

If what they understood isn't even on the same planet as what you thought you said, there is more work to be done. But, and this is very important, do **_not_** begin by blaming either side for the misunderstanding.

"Meghan would give us instructions and then get all upset because we didn't understand what she wanted," retells Daniel, "Rather than allowing us to ask questions or clarify, she'd just shake her hands like they were dirty or something and say things like, 'I'm no good at this,' or 'how can I make you understand?' We always felt like she thought we were dumb, when really she just wasn't clear. What really sucked is that a 5-minute meeting would drag into a 20-minute waste of time, and we still didn't know what she wanted us to do."

If you tell your team they're idiots, they will shut down. If you tell the team you're an idiot, they will simply agree. No one is an idiot solely because there is a misunderstanding. Focusing on blame over understanding is like throwing rocks at an auto accident. You're voicing your disapproval, but you are not helping the situation.

Take the time to listen – really listen – to what they are hearing. Re-explain, redefine, and then ask them to repeat. Try different angles, use all the learning styles (audio, visual, kinesthetic), and be patient.

## STEP THREE: CLARIFY

In the paper-folding exercise, we learn that simply allowing clarifying questions along the way greatly increases the team's ability to succeed. We routinely see 80-100% improvement in achieving matching snowflakes.

Often, these clarifying questions go back and forth:

"Tear the corner."

"Which one?"

"The top right."

"Which way should the fold be facing first?"

"Which fold?"

"The big one, with no open edges."

"Face it toward the ceiling."

...and so on.

This clarifying process may seem agonizing at first, but once you and your team develop a pattern of trust, you will find that you get better at communicating with each other and the process becomes quicker. Both accuracy and morale will soar.

If there is a gross misunderstanding, this is the opportunity to get it straightened out. Clarify the objectives and instructions. The best thing you can do is keep it simple. No one does well under fluffy-bunny, touchy-feely, fuzzy ideas with no clear purpose or end point. Yes, you want to promote creativity, but it will actually be squashed if there are no boundaries.

"George said that we'd all meet at the Sydney Botanical Gardens," remembers Quinn, "That's like, 75 acres! When we started asking where, exactly, he said, 'Somewhere in the middle.' Ummm...what? Most of us didn't even bother trying and just took the day off – it's not like we'd find each other in time. He did the same thing to us two years ago, 'Meet me at Seattle Center,' he says. We're based in Milwaukee; we had no idea how vast that place was. It took us all day and most of our cell minutes to find each other. He never even apologized, just acted like we should be able to read his mind. Did he learn? No. Idiot. He does this at work all the time, too. I swear, we never hit a deadline."

Instructions must not only be clear, but specific. If your vision does not clearly match your team's, you will never arrive at the same place.

"Tia gave me a pile of bills and told me to process them," muses James, "I was just learning the system, so I asked a lot of questions and slowly built up speed. She was very patient, and never gave me any feedback, good or bad. I felt that no news was good news, so I just kept doing what I was told. Two weeks later, she fired me. She said that I needed to process 100 pieces a day and I was only at 75. What the hell? Why didn't she just say so? If I knew what my goal was, I would have been working toward that from the get-go!"

No news is never good news.

The most important takeaway from this step is that feedback must come EARLY and OFTEN. If something is going well, let that person know they are on the right track. They will continue with confidence. If something is going awry – don't let it get worse! A course correction early on will save you both time and headaches later.

The thing that both saddens and frustrates me is how often a truly good employee is groomed for failure by poor communication or lack of feedback. Are you firing your best talent because you aren't letting them know what their objectives are? What made you hire them in the first place? If you saw potential there, and they are not living up to it, then it is your lack of clear communication that created an environment where they cannot be challenged and succeed.

If you have employees that aren't meeting expectations, first ensure that those expectations are clear on both sides. Then, clarify the repercussions – good and bad.

## CLEAR REPERCUSSIONS

> *Repercussions are serious and they will take you places.*
> ~ Bryan Clay

Again, listening plays an important role in establishing the consequences of performance, good and bad. On one hand, you must make it clear what will happen if each team member does not meet the demands of their position. On the other hand, you must motivate them when they are doing well to continue to do so.

You have already set clear objectives and ensured understanding. You are all working toward the same end. Now, clearly define what success looks like and the opportunities it will open to them.

Next, clearly define the repercussions should they fail to meet expectations.

Finally, stick to it.

Never make promises you cannot or do not intend to keep. If you have reprimanded an employee and told them that they will face termination should they fail to improve – mean it. Do it.

Similarly, if you promise time off, a promotion, training, or any other reward for meeting expectations – mean it. Do it.

People want to be led by someone they can trust. People want role models, and they want to feel like they are part of something positive where their opinions matter and their work means something.

Remember, your ability to trust and be trustworthy is the strongest asset to your leadership. You will garner a reputation based on your actions, so make them consistent, honest, and fair.

Once you've created the positive environment where your team feels safe to learn and grow, prepare them for that growth by setting clear goals.

## S.W.I.F.T. GOAL SETTING

> *What you get by achieving your goals is not as important as what you become by achieving your goals.*
> ~ Henry David Thoreau

Most leaders have heard of S.M.A.R.T. goals – how to create a goal that is more likely to be met by being:

- **S**pecific
- **M**easurable
- **A**ssignable
- **R**ealistic
- **T**ime related

If the words look a bit different than what you've seen before, it's because they've been used, abused, swapped, rehashed, and re-credited for decades. The acronym first appeared in the November 1981 issue of Management Review in the article, "There's a S.M.A.R.T. Way to Write Management's Goals and Objectives," co-authored by George Doran, Arthur Miller, and James Cunningham.

This tried-and-true method is a very good way to set objectives for your team and/or an individual. It covers all the basics that a goal must have in order to be met. But, it is more than 30 years old. Perhaps it's time for something new.

Frankly, I need my objectives to be crystal clear – with all the repercussions spelled out and visualization worked in. I like to plan to succeed but not be afraid to take risks. I like to celebrate more often. Plus, it's a new millennium in which things move at a much quicker pace. For these reasons, my goals are S.W.I.F.T. goals:

- **S**pecific
- **W**ritten
- **I**ncremental
- **F**ailure-forward
- **T**ime-sensitive

## SPECIFIC

It is essential that any goal is very specific – how else will you know what you are trying to achieve? Spare nothing in detailing what, exactly, the objective is and how it will look once it's achieved. Visualize success and what it will mean, once met.

All of those things in the S.M.A.R.T. goals should be covered here: How will it be measured? Who owns it and all the parts of it when? Is it realistic, given current resources?

Then, take it yet another step and ask those tough questions like:

- What new resources will we need to continue down this path?
- Will there be a significant paradigm shift once this goal is achieved? How will we handle that?
- How will it ultimately affect the team? The company? Our customers?
- What's in it for me?

Never forget an individual's motivation when setting objectives for the team – and vise-versa!

## WRITTEN

This is a crucial step that too many goal-setters skip. Since I've talked about dogs quite a bit, allow me to say that, when it comes to goals, I'd rather be a Retriever than just a Setter!

While the often-cited Harvard study showing massive income differences between those who did and didn't write down their goals is actually an urban legend, there are other studies out there that back up the theory nonetheless. What's more, many of them show that the combination of writing down goals and having an accountability partner significantly increased the success rate.

That's why we're adding the S.W.I.F.T. method to the Battle Plan – you and the employee in question will sign it, thus holding each other accountable to follow it.

You cannot afford to leave your goals to chance! Write them down. Be accountable.

## INCREMENTAL

If you have a giant, big-picture goal, break it down into smaller, incremental goals so that you can not only believe in each goal (they're not too big), but you get to celebrate more often! When you achieve a goal, it's time to celebrate. Then, you set your next goal. You'll find that getting to the next level is more fun and reaching the ultimate goal this way ends up *SWIFTer* than slogging through to an overwhelmingly huge goal.

For instance, there was a dark time in my life when I weighed over 400 lbs. Of course I wanted to lose weight. When I took care of all the medical blocks that prevented weight loss, I had no excuses. I had to set a specific goal. But, the goal of losing 250 pounds, was just too big – too unrealistic for me to grasp. Setting goals that are not believable is setting yourself up for quitting, that is, if you ever get started.

Make the goals incremental, but not so small that they're silly. In my case, to set a goal to lose 5 pounds was too small. I could lose that much in sweat just walking to the mailbox, only to gain it back by rehydrating. A more realistic increment for me was 50.

Of course these increments will vary by the person and the situation. If you only have 20 pounds to lose, the first 5 or 10 would actually be a motivator for you where it wasn't for me.

Set the increments so that they will stretch your abilities but not break your spirit. Then, celebrate, celebrate, celebrate!

## FAILURE-FORWARD

Most goal setting programs don't allow for failures as part of the process. This is short-sighted, because failure is where the learning happens. If you fail along the way, it doesn't mean you stop working toward the goal altogether, it simply means that you get the opportunity to learn something new and that it's time to reassess. Make corrective adjustments and then get back into action. This is failing forward.

John C. Maxwell, author of the book *Failing Forward* said "The greatest mistake we make is living in constant fear that we will make one."

So, instead of worrying about failing – we're adding it to the equation.

## TIME-SENSITIVE

This is where S.M.A.R.T. and S.W.I.F.T. circle back on each other. A someday, pie-in-the-sky timeframe is bogus: Be proactive and set a timeframe to achieve the objective _and_ a timeframe to celebrate that achievement.

Create a sense of urgency that spurs action. This does not mean the 'missed a deadline and now we're all going to panic' type of urgency. This is an enthusiastic, 'we're moving toward a common end that will benefit us all' type of urgency, otherwise known as 'enthusiasm.'

If using this for an individual's Battle Plan, urgency is important because the ultimate goal is to bring that person back on as a productive member of the team and hopefully as a happier employee.

When implementing S.W.I.F.T. goals, you'll find that it helps to appreciate the members of your team simply for being members of a dynamic, highly-achieving team.

## APPRECIATE

> *You have to, in your own life, get people to want to*
> *work with you and want to help you. The*
> *organizational chart, in my opinion, means very little.*
> *I need my bosses' goodwill, but I need the goodwill of*
> *my subordinates even more.*
> ~ *Lloyd Blankfein*

Letting your employees know you appreciate them is an ongoing task. This is different from giving them kudos for a job well done (we'll talk about that later), this is simply letting them know that they matter. When employees feel appreciated, they will be more loyal to the company and to you.

The best way to do this is to listen.

In the busy, tech-driven world of today, many of us have completely lost the ability to truly be present and listen to another human being. Correcting this will go a long way in your communication efforts.

Your team is made up of many personality types, each with different motivators behind their desire to achieve. Cluing in to these different types will help you better engage with and encourage the individuals on your team without leaving anyone out.

Creating team traditions will lead to a culture of inspired energy and fun. This release is sorely needed, no matter how serious the business is. It builds character and team spirit, making your department run much smoother.

## DEVELOPING LISTENING SKILLS

> *I remind myself every morning: Nothing I say this day*
> *will teach me anything. So if I'm going to learn, I must*
> *do it by listening.*
> ~ Larry King

We've been hearing since the dawn of time, but it's only since we've created shared languages that we've had to really learn how to listen. After a couple of millennia, you'd think we'd be better at it. Instead, we are inventing newer and more exotic ways to misunderstand and ignore one another.

Listening – really listening – shows respect. It develops trust. It enables you to deliver clearer instructions, correct mistakes, and get to the bottom of the biggest issues. All told, working to listen and understand shows that you appreciate the communicator as a human being and, in this case, a viable asset to your team.

## INTERNAL DISTRACTIONS

Before we delve too deep, let's discuss those internal distractions: Your personal filters. These include stereotypes, assumptions, judgments, and emotions. All of these get in the way of full understanding. They run around your brain as internal distractions, taking your focus off of the speaker and back onto you, your beliefs, and your preconceived notions about that speaker.

If you want to be a leader, you must leave those things behind.

As a leader you may have people on your team that you don't particularly like. You may have to lead and inspire people of different backgrounds, religious beliefs, political stripes, sizes, shapes, and colors. If any of these bother you, get over it. Your petty prejudices have no place in the professional world.

When you pre-judge or discount a member of your team, you are missing out on the truth of who they are and what they can contribute. You are stifling creativity and you are decreasing your trustworthiness.

On top of all that, you may get emotional as you carry on an internal dialog looking for ways to disagree with someone you pre-judged. Take a deep breath. Again, check those prejudices at the door. Respond to facts, not emotions.

Do your best to practice empathy – NOT SYMPATHY. Remember the Attention Spectrum? Pity is negative attention. Giving people pity is like feeding deer – they will keep coming back for more, and they will breed. They will suck up all of your resources until there is nothing left but dependency.

Do your best to understand what the person is going through, but do not console. If they go on and on about personal issues, ask them point blank how this affects the team and if it's appropriate for the workplace.

Do not apologize for their issues, it has nothing to do with you. If you apologize, you are accepting blame and they will be more than happy to find a way to blame you, no matter how creative.

Everyone goes through difficult times now and then, so watch that you aren't slipping into pity mode and offering them special treatment. Be fair. Offer them resources such as access to your EAP (Employee Assistance Program) or treatment, if they need it, and then give them the power to take care of the problem. Hold them accountable for their own issues. Your job is not to counsel your team, it is to lead.

## ASSUME BEST INTENTIONS

There may be times when someone is having difficulty communicating what they mean and they say something that sounds untoward or even mean. You may take offense. Don't take something that isn't offered!

So often, people steal offense in a situation when none was presented – the speaker was simply not clear. Why steal something you don't even want?

It is very rare that someone will purposely be cruel. They may be frustrated, upset, even very angry. They may say things they don't mean because they feel they are not being heard, or they may try to say something that is on their mind and bungle it horribly.

Assume best intentions. When you are speaking to your team as a group and someone speaks up, assume they are speaking for the good of the group. From that perspective, what they say often looks quite different than what it would if you assumed they are trying to sabotage the meeting or shoot you down.

If what someone says does sound off-kilter, question for clarity.

QUESTION FOR UNDERSTANDING

A large part of listening involves clarification, particularly in our diverse workforce where many cultures have different learning and communication styles. The only way you can really understand what someone is explaining is to ask questions along the way. Don't be shy about asking for clarification or repeating back what you heard, in your own words, so that the speaker knows both that you are listening and that you understand what they are trying to convey.

It works both ways. When you are speaking or giving directions, ask clarifying questions as you go along, too.

For goodness sake, don't ask, "Do you have any questions." You will seldom get anything but crickets. It's the rare individual who is willing or able to put themselves in the spotlight and ask a question, no matter how poignant.

Make your call for questions specific – by asking a question yourself. When you ask targeted questions, you'll get more involvement and will spur new questions.

Also, stay away from "Do you understand?" That puts someone on the spot – and it insults them. All you will get is a room full of bobble-heads as they nod along – even if they are totally confused. Why would anyone admit to being the dummy who doesn't get it?

Even if you're discussing something one-on-one, you wouldn't answer with, "No. I don't understand you. Please be clearer." If you did, it still wouldn't help because the speaker won't understand where you got lost and will assume you simply weren't listening.

If you want to steer clear of putting folks on the spot, let them know ahead of time that you will be asking questions along the way. This is called "pre-calling," and is very effective. The trick is to use "I" language and make it sound like they are doing you a favor by listening and asking questions. An example would be, "This is a very important project and has various technical components, so I will be asking some questions along the way to make sure I am being clear."

By pre-calling the questions, no one feels picked on. By using "I" language, you're letting them know that you don't think they're dopes, but that you truly want to make sure you're communicating effectively. Then, when you do call on someone to ask a question, you're simply enlisting their help.

This works to your advantage in another way, as well. If you ask someone a question like, "Bob, would you repeat, in your words, what I explained about the Jones account?" Bob will not only let you know if he understood, but by putting it in his words, he'll help the rest of the team by explaining it a different way. If Bob gets it, he'll help the rest of the team that didn't get it the first time. If Bob doesn't get it, he'll start asking questions that will help clarify it.

## BODY LANGUAGE

Scientists say that nonverbal communication makes up between 55-93% of comprehension. While that is a wide margin, it is still larger than words or voice quality combined. There are many nonverbal clues that we give or unconsciously translate as we speak. Your posture, gestures, and facial expressions can completely skew your message, if you let them.

For instance, if the person across from you sits with their arms crossed the entire meeting, you may assume they are disagreeing with you or judging you harshly. It may affect your ability to continue speaking as you wonder and worry what they're thinking. Sadly, they may just be chilly.

Have you done this to someone else inadvertently? How do you get around something like that? What if you really are cold?

Just like pre-calling for questions, you may be able to pre-call for certain gestures. You could simply say, as you walk in the room, "My, it's chilly in here," as you cross your arms to keep warm.

I once had a woman who sat in the very front row of one of my presentations and winked at me the whole first half of the program. During the break, she confided that her contact was driving her crazy and she was on her way to the bathroom to see if she could fix it.

I told her I appreciated the heads up, because, while she was an attractive lady, she certainly wasn't my type.

We were able to laugh about it later. I was able to get over my concern about her actions before I knew what was going on because, rather than make a quick judgment, I try to give people the benefit of the doubt. They tend to live up to the good, rather than any harsh judgments I can concoct.

Some other common non-verbals to be wary of, particularly if you are the one talking:

Rubbing your face as you speak is perceived as being deceitful (lying). Similarly, keeping your hands near or over your mouth portrays that you are uncertain. Watch politicians answer (or avoid) questions – see if they don't put a finger or two near their mouths each time. You may just have an itchy beard, but I'm interpreting your words as lies.

If you've ever watched a child read her report or deliver lines in a school pay, you may have seen her do what we in Toastmasters call "figleafing." When you cover your genitals, you are seen as insecure or extremely defensive. Best to keep your hands to your sides.

In my years of learning sign language (both ASL and SEE), I also learned a little about signing in other countries. For instance, the middle finger in Japanese and a few other Asian sign languages means "brother." We could get in a lot of trouble calling each other brother like that here in the States. While hand shapes and fingers used vary wildly in other country, one finger is universal: the Pointer.

Pointing is, at best, seen as rude. At worst, it conveys anger and/or threatening intentions. When you point at someone, it is like stabbing them in the forehead with that finger. That is why flight attendants will use two fingers or their whole hands to point to the exits and aisles – because even accidentally pointing at another person is seen as offensive.

You can manage this same, aggressive pointing sensation with your voice, too. Without using your finger, if you say "you" in an accusatory manner, it gets the same, bristling reaction as jabbing someone in the forehead with your pointer finger.

Beware the finger!

## EYE CONTACT

In the US, we are extremely good at eye contact. Sometimes too good. Sometimes downright creepy.

We are told from a very young age to make a lot of eye contact with someone when they're talking. But staring is not the right thing to do. It's human nature to look away while speaking or listening. Too much eye contact, and you come across as too intense or downright scary. Too little and you are perceived as submissive or simply not listening.

What do you do to make sure you aren't losing the speaker or completely freaking them out? The simple answer is to try your best to match what they are doing – without mirroring them to the point that they feel you're mocking them. People will generally start a conversation with the amount of eye contact that they are comfortable with. You only need to follow along.

It's not an exact science, so don't get too crazy about trying to be perfect. It's best to just be yourself and not worry about eye contact other than to look at the person who is talking. Your instincts are more honed than you give yourself credit for.

Don't get wrapped up in internal counting or calculations or you won't be listening, and that's more important than anything else.

## ALLOW SILENCE

You do not have to be talking in order to be heard. Humans in general hate silence and tend to fill it in with all sorts of mindless noise. Often, this noise replaces any true communication. Just stop talking already and let someone else get a word in edgewise!

If you ask a specific question and don't get an answer, or you get an evasive answer such as, "I don't know," nod encouragingly and wait. Don't say a word. Just wait with an expectant look on your face as if the next words they say will be brilliant. Most likely, they will be. After a long, awkward silence, they *will* start talking. What comes out at that point is honesty. This works great in interviews and with teenagers, too.

Listen completely before responding. Have you ever asked a question or made a comment that upset the person you're talking to, or they just shut down and gave up trying to talk to you? It was most likely because you weren't listening and you butted in with a non sequitur. You were inside your head formulating your next reply and you missed what was being said. Your reply proved that you hadn't heard them, and they lost trust that you even cared.

If you are a person who tends to stick your foot in your mouth, or you are shy and one of your greatest fears is saying the wrong thing or not knowing what to say at all, don't worry. Stop rehearsing your next comment in your head while the other person is talking. That is actually *why* you've said the wrong thing so many times – you were not paying attention. Please understand that if you listen – really listen – the right words will come when it is your turn to speak.

As someone who has survived domestic violence both as a child and as a battered spouse, I understand that fear firsthand. I know what it feels like to be frightened to speak up. I know what it feels like to be frightened to speak at all. Trust me when I say that if you stop internalizing and start listening, the right words will come. I promise.

## ENCOURAGE THE SPEAKER

When someone else is speaking, use reassuring or leading words to show you are paying attention and to encourage them to continue. "Uh huh...oh...yes...really?" and the like.

Make sure these encouraging sounds match what is being said. It will be very obvious if you are just making noise and not really listening. It can even get you in trouble if your response to a negative comment is an enthusiastic, "Oh, uh-huh."

Do not finish their sentences. Rarely will you finish it with what they intended to say, and it will always frustrate them because it is being dismissive. Let them finish for themselves, even if they're being frustratingly slow. They'll come up to speed once they realize that you are listening and won't discount them, pre-judge them, or cut them off.

## MOTIVATE BY PERSONALITY TYPE

*Reward life skills and personal growth. Good people
do a good job and bad people do a bad job.*
~ Larry Winget

What motivates a person to strive toward success? There is no one answer – and this is wonderful news! Your team should be diverse, as we've clearly illustrated, which means there are many ways to motivate.

Following are the basic types of motivation based on personality type. It's interesting to note that few of them are motivated by money, and none of them are motivated to succeed or excel by fear.

Keep in mind that a person will rarely fall into a single category. You may straddle a couple of them yourself. The idea here is to find the things that will feed the soul of the person you want to inspire. Bear in mind that these are very basic types and not meant to pigeonhole anyone into a particular role. The idea is to get a firmer grasp on what will encourage the different personality types on your team so that you can offer a comprehensive motivational and rewards plan.

## INTRINSIC

Intrinsically motivated people find satisfaction from the inside. They enjoy self-improvement, achievement for achievement's sake, and seek a high level of competence in their interests. They tend to be emotionally invested in their productivity. There are several different types of intrinsically motivated people, here are a few:

### *ALTRUISTICS*

Altruistics seek situations in which they can work toward the greater good. These people will do well in their jobs if they can see how the big picture will help others. They are good to have on outreach teams and like to help their coworkers whenever they can.

Altruistics are motivated by projects and work that fits within their belief systems. They most likely took the position with your company because your vision and mission statements aligned with their own.

### *FUTURE-EMOTIONALS*

Future-Emotionals are always thinking ahead to how they will feel and love to complete something almost as much as they love to start something new. You can recognize them on your team as the ones who completely clean out their "In" and "Out" boxes by close of business every Friday. In fact, they most likely clear off their whole desk and take the glass cleaner to their monitor so that they can come in Monday morning to a fresh, clean desk and a brand-new start.

Future-emotionals do well with cycles and projects with deadlines and hard completion dates. They are demotivated by fuzzy objectives or ongoing projects with no end in sight.

## PROFICIENCY SEEKERS

Proficiency seekers want to be the absolute best at their main interest. They will read, experiment, and seek others who are proficient at the particular skill to learn as much as they can. These are the type that you can give full, unlimited internet access to and find that they do more work-related research than anything else.

Proficiency seekers are motivated by higher learning, typically technical, and can sometimes – not always – be antisocial. However, because they seek to be SMEs (Subject Matter Experts), they are motivated by sharing their wisdom and they make great mentors. If you have someone on your team that you call the "guru" of a particular thing, they are most likely this type.

These are the best people to put in charge of creating SOPs and other documentation that must be very detailed. Be careful, though, because they are demotivated by busywork and can get bored easily if there is no room to grow.

## SELF-IMPROVERS

Self-Improvers are life-long learners who seek improvement for improvement's sake, even if there is absolutely no prize at the end. They are motivated by higher learning, mentorships, and increasing both their proficiency and their self-understanding. They can be spiritual people, but not necessarily.

You can recognize these people on your team by their library of self-help and leadership books. They may seek memberships with organizations like Toastmasters and be subscribers to seminar programs.

Self-improvers are demotivated by excuses or being told they cannot do something. They like to ask questions and will go out of their way to seek understanding on both sides.

## AUTONOMY SEEKERS

Autonomy Seekers are looking to be left alone, for the most part, to do their job and do it well. They enjoy figuring things out for themselves and, while they respond well to private, relevant feedback, they would be mortified to be put in the spotlight.

Autonomy seekers are often viewed as shy people and have no desire whatsoever to be leaders. They are not motivated by money, prizes, or accolades. They simply want to be sure they are on the right track and to be left alone to get done what needs to be done.

This type does well with cycles and clear SOPs. They are self-starters and may tune you out if you over-explain. They are demotivated by unclear expectations and talking about emotions or non-work-related subjects. They often must be coaxed to ask questions.

## EXTRINSIC

Extrinsically motivated people find satisfaction more from outside resources, such as affiliation, power to help or change people or situations, social recognition, and, of course, goodies.

Many extrinsically motivated people get a significant amount of satisfaction from within, as well. They may just be a little louder or flashier about it.

### BLING-SEEKERS

Bling-Seekers, as their name implies, like the finer things in life. They are the rare birds that are truly only motivated by money and the prestige that comes with it. You can recognize these people on you team because they drive a nicer car than you do. They wear name-brand clothing and only the finest jewelry.

Most bling-seekers have a deeper motivation, but this is the one they allow to the surface most often. You may have to do a little bit of digging to find out what else makes them tick.

### POWER LEADERS

Power Leaders are not necessarily the foot-stomping, Napoleonic pains-in-the-ass that their name implies. Most truly desire to be influencers of people and policy – typically for the good. They are motivated by feeling like they are not just in charge, but are inducing change.

The best thing about power leaders is that they are the ones willing to take risks. If you have a difficult or important project that needs a lead, these are the type you want in front, particularly if it means a paradigm shift or surge forward for the organization as a whole. They can work very well with the altruistic types, as long as the project aligns with their values.

## SOCIAL RECOGNITION SEEKERS

Social Recognition Seekers like to be lauded. They tend to be gregarious, outgoing people who can be quite competitive. They love to be the center of attention, but only in a positive light. While these types of people will go out of their way for attention, they will avoid negative attention at all costs.

These people are motivated by awards, including certificates, trophies, and plaques – but only if they are earned. "Participant" certificates and the like are trashed as they mean nothing. Usually, they will not display second- or third-place awards, unless it was an extremely competitive event where few make it to the final round and placing is a major deal.

While social recognition seekers love to be the center of attention, they can actually be introverts at heart. They revel in the spotlight, but often seek quiet time alone afterwards.

These people can be impulsive and quick decision-makers. They make good leaders and generally like people and are good with them. They learn by doing and by getting a lot of feedback along the way. They are demotivated by not being recognized or, at least, heard.

## AFFILIATIVES

Affiliatives are your people people. They love to socialize and meet new folks. They are not necessarily good in groups, and do not tend to be competitive, unless they feel they are being marginalized. They can be name droppers, and revel in pictures of themselves with stars and other brushes with fame. They are fabulous one-on-one and can be very good listeners.

Affiliatives are motivated by who they know. They are good as mentors, and are great ambassadors should you have an outreach program or an artist affiliate program. They get jazzed by rewards such as lunch with the CEO or outings to concerts and the like, particularly if you scored back-stage tickets.

## DIFFER THE MOTIVATION; SURGE THE PRODUCTIVITY

There are many variations within each type listed here, but you can see that each is motivated by very different things. If you offer only raises and promotions as incentives, you will lose more than half of your team – those things simply do not motivate most people.

This also means that you have to take a little time to get to know each member of your team, which is a good thing. Once you've established that trust, you might even ask them, point-blank, what would motivate or encourage their best work.

## CREATE TEAM TRADITIONS

Every team has its own culture which includes little traditions and rituals that help build a foundation of trust, respect, and fun. If you've been focusing too much on the results and not on the people who create those results, then you are missing an opportunity to surge proficiency, creativity, and productivity to the next level.

In short, because you focus only on results, your actual results will suffer.

These little traditions do not have to be expensive, nor do they have to be time-consuming. They only have to be unique and involve the team as a whole. This is also a fantastic way to set the stage for some honest feedback and open communication. Your willingness to be part of the team – not just its fearless leader – shows that you are trustworthy and that you trust your team. Never underestimate the power of human connections.

Traditions that I've experienced include:

- Potlucks
- Monthly barbeques
- Casual Fridays
- Celebrating birthdays
- Roaming trophies
- Open agendas for meetings
- Desk decorating
- Themed days
- Friendly competitions
- Happy Hour
- Ice-cream day

- Visiting the local museum on local's free day (First Friday or similar programs)

Your team will not only enjoy taking a little time away from the daily grind, but they will feel valued. The message you send with these small acts of fun is powerful. It means you see them as people first.

Use the culture of your team to allow these traditions to form naturally. They may grow and morph as the team matures.

# DELEGATE

*The price of greatness is responsibility.*
*~ Winston Churchill*

As a manger, you are given important tasks to complete within a certain amount of time. You are given a team to assist you in this endeavor. Your job is to delegate these tasks in the most useful ways so that each gets done in a timely and efficient manner.

Delegating isn't just doling out random tasks to your staff. If you engage in the "shuffle and pass" type of delegation, you most likely have been met with some resistance at best and abject failure as a norm. This is because you are missing out on a brilliant opportunity.

When you delegate work, think about what strengths and passions each member of your team has. They are not all the same. The tasks you give each person will either energize them or drag them down. Each person will enjoy different things, but what all enjoy is being trusted and treated like a valuable member of the team.

When delegating, give each person a whole task or project – not just piecework. Let them "own" it – which means they may not do it the same way you would. As long as it gets done efficiently and accurately, your concern is not the process by which it is completed. Communicate very clearly what the scope of the task is, and ask questions (or have them explain) along the way so that it is clear you both understand the same thing. If you have an example or SOPs, hand that over. Then, hold them accountable for the results. They will appreciate the trust.

In fact, part of the task may be to have them create that documentation for the next person. This would make it very clear to everyone what the task entails, the best path to follow, and what the best outcome looks like.

Do not be fuzzy about the process or the completed task or you will set your teammates up for failure. Instead, play to win. Offer them the most clear, concise description of the outcome, both desired and required, so that you can cheer them on to success.

Delegating important projects can actually be used as a reward, which is why it is listed under "Motivate." When you delegate an important or highly-visible task to someone on your team you are:

- Showing them you trust their abilities
- Allowing them to be seen by the higher-ups
- Allowing them to take the lead
- Challenging them to greater things
- Giving them an opportunity to learn something new

All of these things are very motivating to someone who wants to excel.

## LET OTHERS LEAD

If you've ever been in a group such as Toastmasters or a church, you know that leadership positions – from the local club or chapter's board to the larger organization itself – are difficult to fill. Why? Because it takes a lot of hard work, knowledge, and diplomacy, which is asking a bit much of a volunteer. The minute you take the position, you are looking for that person you are confident can fill your spot in the next term so that you can start mentoring them right away.

There is a disconnection in the corporate world. Once a leader is in place, he feels he must hang on to his position tooth and nail or else bad things will happen. He won't allow anyone to learn what he does or how he does it because if anyone knew, he'd lose his power. Rather than mentor new leaders, he squashes them. He never realizes that he's only making his and everyone else's job harder.

When you are a true leader (not just a boss), part of your job is to empower those who might be your successors. Not in such a way that they want to overthrow you, but in such a way that they want to *own* their positions. This means giving them specific responsibilities for which they are accountable. Yes, that means letting go of some of your control and allowing others to make decisions, but if you can do that, you actually have better hold of the situation. You might even learn something.

When you allow others to make decisions, they become invested and *own* their positions. When people own their positions, they enjoy feeling responsible for the outcome, and tend to be more in tune with the mission and vision of the entity as a whole. Simply put, they will care more.

When your team cares more, they produce more.

When your team produces more, you look good.

When you look good, you have more opportunities such as raises, promotions, and killer recommendations. At that point, it's sure a good idea to have folks in place that you'd want to replace you, especially when you might end up their supervisor again in your new position.

How do you empower your team? Part of it is simply allowing them to earn your trust. Start with their basic duties, then give them a little more responsibility. It doesn't have to be giant steps, just enough that they can handle. When they're successful, celebrate that success in a way that fits the person and the task, and then trust them with more.

Do you have a project that needs special attention? Form a mini-team, complete with team leader, to get it done in record time. Set clear, measurable objectives and then *let go*. Check in at appropriate times. Help only when asked. Above all, listen. If something is awry, they'll tell you.

Is there someone who excels at the daily tasks that others ignore or forget? Ask them to create a program that would help the others either achieve them more quickly or automate. Let them run it.

Allowing the natural leaders on your team to increase their leadership skills ensures your leadership is lauded. When the apprentice becomes the master, you have achieved your ultimate objective.

## CHECK IN

> *The single biggest problem in communication is the*
> *illusion that it has taken place.*
> ~ George Bernard Shaw

You've learned to avoid micromanaging – but that does not mean to avoid your staff altogether. Make it a custom to meet one-on-one with each member of your staff for no other reason than to check in. Offer them your time and insight to answer questions, clarify objectives, and even complain, if they must. If you're unclear about what to do here, the most important thing that you can do is to shut up.

Seriously, just listen. It's what every human being on the planet desires most: to be heard. If no one has ever offered you a brilliant suggestion, it is only because you have been unable or unwilling to listen. Your team is smarter than you think.

## THE CUPCAKE REVOLUTION

This is a challenge I offer to all of my participants in my Coaching and Mentoring for Leaders class. As stated earlier, most managers in the working world are seen mainly as disciplinarians. Whenever we send an email or leave a sticky note on someone's work station to come see us, it means that they are in trouble. They make the walk of shame to our office or cubicle as if they are nine years old and got called to the principal's office. Meanwhile, everyone points and laughs, as they know that poor person is about to be chewed out, at best, possibly written up, and fired, at worst.

Let's change this mentality.

I learned as a foster and volunteer at an animal shelter that many dogs are destroyed due to food aggression because they are deemed unadoptable. This breaks my heart, as this is an easily corrected behavior.

Most strays aggressively protect their food because they've gone hungry at some point. Their owners' or fosters' knee-jerk reaction is to take the food away. What does this do? It encourages the dog to protect its food even more fiercely, which may lead to snapping, even biting, should you approach the animal as it is eating.

How do you break them of the fear that their food will be taken?

Feed them a little, then, as they are eating, add food to the dish.

Do this consistently for every feeding and, after a while, they will no longer associate someone approaching them as they are eating with losing their sustenance. (*For more information on Systematic*

*Desensitization and Counterconditioning, please visit the ASPCA website.*)

Please understand, again, that I am not comparing you or anyone on your team to dogs. I am simply saying that it is time to desensitize and counter-condition them from believing that you are the distributor of punishment.

This is where cupcakes come in.

Throughout the next year, send emails or leave sticky notes that simply ask to come see you. When they make the walk of shame to your office, simply give them a cupcake (or something as fun and non-threatening), and send them on their way.

Graduate up to asking them how their day is, and listening. Sprinkle in some anecdotes, or maybe some questions about their latest project. Again, more listening.

Soon, being called to meet with you will no longer be a negative experience. You will be able to comment, question, even offer course corrections now and then, without all the fear and loathing of 'visiting the boss.'

This will open up the lines of communication like never before. Finally, you are no longer the disciplinarian or counsellor; you are a peer in a leadership position who has their best interests at heart. They will no longer respond to your presence with aversion or diversion.

## KEEP BUILDING

> *Without leaps of imagination or dreaming, we lose*
> *the excitement of possibilities. Dreaming, after all, is a*
> *form of planning.*
> ~ *Gloria Steinem*

Building a team is not an event – it is an ongoing activity. Yes, you may have hired the perfect group of people for the roles you need filled, but that does not make them a team. No sports team ever won by just showing up the day of the game. They practiced, learned each other's strengths and weaknesses, figured out how to work around or improve the deficits, and practiced some more.

There are at least a bajillion teambuilding programs out there, any of which may work – but only if your teammates already see themselves as a team. If they bicker, backstab, circumvent, tattle, avoid, or sabotage – clean house.

All of those teambuilding exercises revolve around one thing: Trust.

## BUILDING TRUST

Trust is difficult to build, but so easy to destroy that it's easier to learn all the ways you can destroy it and work to avoid those practices. So often it is assumed that building trust should come naturally to a leader, but trustworthiness is a learned trait, not an inherent one.

It really comes down to your communication style. People, particularly those you are in a leadership role with, will believe what you say. If they find out later that you were less than honest, they will give up on you. They want to be able to trust you and will feel betrayed if they learn that they cannot depend on you to be truthful. So, say what you mean and mean what you say.

Watch those absolutes:

- Always
- Never
- Nobody / No one
- Everybody
- All
- Every (and the redundant, "every single solitary...")
- None
- Can't

If you tell someone, "You never do _____," and they have so much as halfway attempted to do it even once, then in their eyes, you are liar.

Exaggerations are great for storytelling but have no place in teambuilding.

If you positively, absolutely, 100% want to guarantee that someone will push a button, put a sign above it that says, "You can't push this button."

Normal human beings will go out of their way to prove you wrong.

But, don't think that using reverse psychology will work, either. Remember, you are a leader and your team desires to look up to you. If you start telling them they can't do something, they may resent – even hate you for it – but they will eventually believe you.

Why on earth would you want to stifle their initiative?

If something seems impossible, ask for their opinions. Allow them to be creative. Value their ideas. Don't just encourage creativity – EXPECT it! People will live up to your expectations.

Give them credit where credit is due. Taking recognition for someone else's work or ideas may make you look good in the short run, but it always comes back to bite you in the long haul. It certainly destroys your credibility with your team, and they will stop giving you ideas altogether. If you are an idea stealer, what will you do when those ideas dry up?

When you give your team credit for their ingenuity, you look like a genius. People will look up to you as the one who mentored the best and the brightest. They will trust you as the one who fosters creativity and passes the praise to those who deserve it. These are promotable traits. Build them.

## DO NOT SUFFOCATE

> *Efficiency is doing things right. Effectiveness is doing*
> *the right things.*
> ~ *Peter Drucker*

Micromanaging is one of the top three complaints of employees worldwide. Come on, we're all adults here, let's act like it. If you feel that you have to breathe down your employees' necks and control every tiny detail of their work day, then you have a really poor perception of both their and your own abilities.

Your entire job boils down to clearly communicating the mission and goals of the company, each person's duties, and how they fit into that scope. Then, back off. Let them do it. No, they might not do it exactly as you would do it. They might do it more efficiently, more creatively, or more cost-effectively. Back off and watch just how ingenious your team can be, when allowed.

If they truly do not get it, reevaluate your communication efforts. Try again a different way.

If they really are idiots, reassess again. Is it even possible to have hired an entire team of imbeciles? What are the odds? Think back to your previous jobs. What made you leave? Were they all idiots, too?

How about your manager – is he a dumdum? Your previous manager? The one before that?

Hmm...what is the common denominator here? If no one has ever understood you, whose fault is that?

Hint: It's not them, it's you.

## WHAT MICROMANAGING IS NOT

If you have a team that has faced some terrible bosses – including you – then you may be met with some whining that anything you do is "micromanaging." To help you understand your true role, here is what micromanaging is not:

CLARIFYING your expectations, when done as two-way communication to ensure understanding, is not micromanaging. While you may get some pushback if you've never done it before, in the long run, it will be appreciated and you will find that with better understanding comes more efficient and accurate results.

GIVING DIRECTION to someone who is struggling or who needs some guidance, if done with understanding and allowing for questions and cooperation, is good practice. If you have been an invisible or too-busy boss, this may be misunderstood at first. Tread lightly, but be persistent. Help them find their way, then back off.

EVALUATING performance – *early* and *often* – as long as it's done in a constructive, forward-thinking way, may also be met with resistance if you've not been able to successfully do this in the past. Keep those lines of communication open and offer lots of positive, specific praise and encouragement.

When you are able to **cultivate** and **motivate** you team to greater vision and performance, it's time to celebrate!

## CELEBRATE

*As we express our gratitude, we must never forget*
*that the highest appreciation is not to utter words,*
*but to live by them.*
~ *John F. Kennedy*

Your job is not to babysit, your job is to create new leaders and ensure autonomy for your team. An excellent leader is always an effective coach on some level. Coaches develop talent, not squash it.

One of the most common misconceptions that leaders have about their teammates is that each person recognizes his worth or can see all possible growth opportunities. Generally (and sadly,) they don't. This is not because they are not bright – it's because our culture discourages it. Success is against our current common culture. Celebrating one's success is even more taboo.

Go against common culture, and you'll be uncommonly successful.

Talk is cheap. While you will learn how to best communicate appreciation and room for improvement, keep in mind that there are many ways to actually show people that they matter. Actions will always speak louder than words.

Also remember, you *are* the example. You teach others how you want to be treated. So if you do not appreciate your team, they will not appreciate you.

Create community and build that camaraderie by taking the time to do things that are people-focused. People don't care about statistics and bottom lines, people care about people.

## Constructive Feedback

> *We all need people who will give us feedback. That's*
> *how we improve.*
> *~ Bill Gates*

People toss around the word "criticism" and act like putting the word "constructive" in front of it somehow makes it something that it's not. The dictionary definition defines criticism as, "The act of passing judgment as to something's merit." Do you like being judged? Do you like being classified by another person, having them decide your merit?

Me, either. Criticism does not construct anything.

Instead, let's talk about feedback. This is a two-way street, so while you are offering feedback, remember all of those listening skills you are developing and honing.

For feedback to be beneficial, it must be:

- Early & Often
- Specific & Singular
- Relevant & Actionable

## EARLY & OFTEN

*Feedback is the breakfast of champions.*
*~ Ken Blanchard*

If there are only two things you remember about feedback make it this: Feedback must be EARLY and OFTEN in order for it to mean anything. Remember The Puppy Principle? If you punish your puppy after the fact, he truly has no idea why. People are the same way. If you spend more time reminding people of whatever it is you are talking about than you do actually talking about the issue — good or bad — than you are too late. The feedback is no longer relevant to the moment.

## PUBLIC VS. PRIVATE

This is not the old "Praise in public, criticize in private" rhetoric. The main reason being that criticism does not work – public or not.

Criticizing someone in front of their peers is ineffective. Even if you have a perfectly valid point, all they hear is that you desired to humiliate them. It does not motivate, never has, and never will. The closest thing you will ever see is that person straightening out just long enough to find another job. Usually what you'll see is a team that avoids you and each other with each member just trying to not get singled out.

For now, we'll overlook the fact that straight criticism only makes things worse. Telling someone what went wrong without giving the tools to correct is useless. You're just being mean. If you do it in front of their peers, you're being sadistic. Those witnessing your little display are embarrassed, not motivated.

## EARLY

This does **_not_** mean that if you need to correct someone's work or reprimand them for doing something wrong that you can simply call them into your office when you get around to it.

If you can catch someone in the act of doing something worth mentioning – good or bad – take them aside and discuss it while it's fresh.

Given the overabundance of ineffective managers, workplace culture dictates that if you hear nothing, you're either doing fine or you're about to be thwacked on your annual review. Your only motivation at that point is to just keep on keeping on and hope it won't be too bad.

Meanwhile, you do not excel and you do not strive to reach your full potential because you simply do not know what it is or even if it's allowed. You do just enough to stay under the radar.

No news is *never* good news.

Praise, much like correction, should come early and often.

## OFTEN

This might mean going out of your way to notice the good things. Make the effort. People want encouragement. Positive reinforcement *works*. Don't wait for some set time to deliver feedback. Even if it's informal, it's valuable. Don't hold back.

## SPECIFIC & SINGULAR

> *Regular feedback is one of the hardest things to drive through an organization.*
> ~ Kenneth Chenault

It doesn't help to praise or critique in generalities. Often, what you mean to convey is misunderstood, so you're wasting your breath. Folks aren't mind readers. The more specific you are, the better they will understand and the more invested they'll be going forward.

Let's look at some actual examples of ineffective feedback and see how we can use the above principles to make them constructive. We'll start with negative feedback:

"Someone said you were rude, and they were upset. You need to work on your attitude."

There are three glaring issues with the above comment. First of all, you are bringing in a third party. If that person isn't present or willing to be named, they are irrelevant to the conversation at hand. In fact, it is often the case that that person doesn't even exist, and, trust me, this ploy will be found out. You lose credibility and the person does not feel any change is needed because you are making something up at worst, or bowing to the tattletale at best.

Second, it is not specific. Rude is subjective. One person's rude is another person's busy. Rude to whom in what way, when? What does upset mean? Furious? Frightened? Knocked over? How can you fix something if it's not clear what's broken?

Finally, it does no good to discuss "attitude" with anyone other than yourself. The only attitude you can control is your own.

Speaking of attitude with anyone else will only put them on the defensive. Imagine someone sticking their finger in your face and telling you that you have a bad attitude. What is your reaction? What is your response?

I bet it's hostile!

How can we make this negative feedback work to mutually benefit you and the employee?

To demonstrate this process, we'll walk through an example.

I once had a difficult employee we'll call Bart. Bart was an incredibly intelligent, quick-witted guy. He had superior technical skills and could really bang out some fabulous work, when he was motivated to do so.

He tended to be sarcastic, however, and he focused his wry humor toward minorities, even though Bart was a minority himself. Bart found a way to insult everyone around him regardless of background. I believe he wasn't even aware that he was being offensive – he thought he was being funny.

Bart also had issues with taking ownership. He didn't like to admit when he made a mistake and would find someone to blame whenever something went wrong – even if he was the only one involved in the project.

Finally, Bart could be kind of a bully. When he felt he was cornered or not getting his way, he'd use backhanded compliments and mock announcements to try to pit people against each other.

How are we going to help Bart?

## BE SPECIFIC

You can only comment on what you know for sure. Do not bring in third parties. If you hear from someone else that something is awry, you may have to do some investigation on your own to see if you can identify the behavior first-hand.

It may well be that you're dealing with a tattle-tale just trying to get someone in trouble. If it's an isolated incident and the person complaining is actually the injured party, bring the two together for mediation. It may very well be a personality clash that can be worked out.

If it actually is an issue of repeated, poor behavior that must be corrected, focus on that. Remember, focus on a *behavior* not an *attitude*.

Now you've got something specific to discuss.

Before I could talk to Bart, I had to see his actions for myself. In this case, it wasn't too difficult. I knew of all his shortcomings, but I had to decide what we would address first.

## BE SINGULAR

If there is a huge laundry list of issues with this person, bombarding them with all of them at once will only make things worse. They will simply feel that you don't like them or are picking on them. Instead, pick a single behavior that must be addressed. Do your best to prioritize so that the one you pick first will take care of several related behaviors. Once you see improvement, celebrate it. Let that person know that you have noticed. That is a very important part of any disciplinary action – improvement must be acknowledged or it will not be lasting.

Then, if there are still other behaviors that must be addressed, the person in question will be more open to them. One at a time.

In Bart's case, I believe he used his sarcasm as a way to cover his insecurities – but of course I couldn't tell him that, because it would seem that I was attacking his attitude. Instead, I chose a specific behavior to address because it would take care of the bullying, and may even tap into the responsibility issues.

## Relevant & Actionable

> *The praise that comes from love does not make us vain, but more humble.*
> *~ James M. Barrie*

For feedback to be worth anything it must be relevant to the time and the issue at hand and it must be actionable. The 'woulda coulda shoulda's' will bury you and your team in regrets. Instead, discuss what can be done to make things better in the future, whether that's what can be avoided or fixed or simply improved.

Back to the issue with Bart:

## MAKE IT RELEVANT

When you get a person to believe they're helping, you are removing the personal judgment aspect. People have a natural desire to be helpful. Build on that.

I enlisted Bart's help.

"Bart, I need your help. You've probably felt the dip in morale lately. You are a really funny guy, and I appreciate your efforts to lift the mood. Keep up the jokes. I have noticed that you can be sarcastic. (Here I listed three specific incidents that I witnessed so that he knew I had heard him and what I meant by sarcasm.) I'd really appreciate it if you would restrain from sarcasm, specifically, because not everyone understands that you are joking. We have a very diverse team, so please keep that in mind – no racial or off-color comments. I trust you'd appreciate the same from the rest of us."

## MAKE IT ACTIONIONABLE

Remember the Puppy Principle? The action you offer here is the alternative behavior that is desired. It must be clearly stated, even demonstrated, if possible. It must also be clear what the repercussions are both if met or ignored.

"That joke you told on Monday about the duck and the senator was hilarious! I don't know where you came up with it, Bart, but I'd love to hear more like that.

"Also, I overheard when you told Mindy that you appreciated her work on the Gillian report. I could tell that made her day. It means a lot to others when you take the time to appreciate them."

I told Bart that we were getting together a "Fun Committee" – a way to lift the moods of his coworkers by planning fun events and outings, and that he would be a good addition to the group. "In fact, you might consider being the chair, but that means you'd have to take the heat if there's any issues."

Finally, I told Bart that sarcastic, aggressive, and racist remarks were, in fact, bullying and would not be tolerated. He agreed.

When I saw improvement, I made sure I let Bart know – early and often.

Now, let's look at positive feedback:

"Good job today," while meant as a compliment, is actually useless and can be seen as flippant or condescending. It's empty praise that truly doesn't inspire any other action.

Instead, try being more precise and/or detailed, "Good call on the Jones account this afternoon, Barbara. They are an important client and your idea made them excited to move forward with the project."

The above example specified not just that Barbara did a good thing, but why you appreciated it and how it supported the mission of the organization. It's motivating praise, because now Barbara will be on the lookout for things that can impress other important clients.

It's also empowering, as Barbara was given the chance to speak freely and offer up an idea that was not only heard, but utilized.

One more component that must not be overlooked: Barbara was called by name. Using someone's name when delivering a positive message is like music to their ears. It shows that you recognize them as a person, not just a worker.

Remember, this applies to the acknowledgement of corrective action, too, "Bart, I saw how hard you worked on the ice-cream social. Both Lin and Sol were thrilled that you offered sugar-free and dairy-fee alternatives. That was very thoughtful, thank you.

"I've also noticed that you've been working to reign in the sarcasm, and it's made a difference. From the work that you and Peggy did on the Yancy report, I can see you have been able to collaborate much more effectively."

Bart continued to improve and eventually moved into a higher-paid position where he did quite well. The rest of the team noticed his efforts, too, and became more trusting of each other, thus becoming more efficient. Our team won a service award from the CEO that year.

## MEANINGFUL PRAISE

> *The more credit you give away, the more will come*
> *back to you. The more you help others, the more they*
> *will want to help you.*
> ~ Brian Tracy

Praise can take you and your team to the next level of effectiveness, but it must be meaningful. Piling on platitudes is every bit as demoralizing as ignoring your team all together.

Part of being able to offer meaningful praise is trusting your team to deliver. If you've offered clear and concise instruction, then you can back off and let them do what they do best. Meanwhile, you should praise them along the way so they know they're on the right track.

We are creative beings. We cannot work in a vacuum and assume that everything is just fine with no feedback. It's tempting to leave the steady producer alone, but they may very well be creating all sorts of scenarios as to why you're not encouraging them. Don't let your top performer fall prey to insecurities. Present them with meaningful praise whenever possible!

Meaningful praise should be **consistent**, **commensurate**, and **catching**.

## CONSISTENT

> *The greatest humiliation in life is to work hard on something from which you expect great appreciation and then fail to get it.*
> *~ E. W. Howe*

If you only hear about earth-shattering good deeds, you begin to think the rest do not matter. Recognize daily and ongoing things, as well.

Remember how good it felt to get something special for perfect attendance in school? It still feels good. Loyalty is underrated and shouldn't be. The person who never misses a deadline or always remembers the office birthdays is to be commended.

In the modern office, it seems the only consistent feedback we get is our annual review, and that is rarely good. Break the mold. Offer consistent praise to the point that it is no longer awkward or uncomfortable, but encouraged and expected from and to everyone, including you.

Being consistent means that you don't play favorites or hold back from anyone. Once it's understood that consistent feedback and praise is part of your style, it won't come as such a surprise. In fact, you will find your team moving toward more rewarding behaviors because they are anticipating that praise.

## COMMENSURATE

> *Praise undeserved is satire in disguise.*
> *~ Alexander Pope*

Commensurate is just a fancy way of saying that the punishment matches the crime – or the reward matches the effort.

Be commensurate with the type and amount of praise you give. Don't go ape over everything large and small. Those that do go above and beyond will resent those that just show up. Praise should match effort.

# CATCHING

> *The secret of genius is to carry the spirit of the child into old age, which mean never losing your enthusiasm.*
> ~ Aldous Huxley

Office gossip is a scourge that can never be fully eradicated, so you might as well direct it with positive messages – positive gossip, if you will. This means offering meaningful praise both to the individual and to the whole team about the individual. Each person will have a preference, so make sure you are not embarrassing them.

When you are praising a specific person, others are listening, and it does affect them. If you don't believe that, imagine your parent praising your sibling and never saying a nice thing to or about you.

Foster an environment where each team member feels not only empowered, but encouraged to praise the others.

Instead of (or on top of) a Secret Santa program, try an Anonymous Affirmation program. Let your teammates tell each other how much they value each other. You'll end up with a firestorm of positivity and a genuine desire from the bulk of your team to help each other out.

This is just one idea. Be creative! The more positive gossip you can spread, the less room there is for negative gossip.

## CELEBRATE MISTAKES

*Our greatest glory is not in never failing, but in rising
up every time we fail.*
~ *Ralph Waldo Emerson*

So often our mistakes are rubbed in our faces that we either try to cover them up or we are weighed down by the fear of them. Because of this, we can easily overlook the good that comes from learning through failure. Mistakes shouldn't be avoided – they should be celebrated!

When the dread and tension of failure is lifted, your team will become more open to instruction. They will invite mentoring and partnerships. They will no longer fear feedback, but embrace it for the learning opportunity that it is supposed to be.

"I was drafted onto our bowling league, even though I told everyone over and over that I couldn't bowl," recounts Mélanie. "Seriously, I had never even managed to get a score – I was the queen of the gutter ball. I just knew that they'd all hate me for lowering their score and losing the tournament. I came in dreading to play. I would be a dismal failure and they'd hate me for it.

"I showed up with a rotten attitude. I picked a stock ball because it was pink, I mean, I didn't know any better. I hucked that heavy SOB down the lane, and, sure enough, it went right into the gutter. With dismay, I turned to face my team.

"They all threw their arms in the air and yelled, "GUTTER BALL!!" then danced around and offered me a beer. It was crazy, but it totally alleviated that fear of failure.

"Later in the evening, after several more gutter balls and lots more cheering, I began to ask questions about bowling. Did you know that bowling balls come in different weights and the finger holes come in different sizes? They helped me pick a ball that was four pounds lighter and that I could get all my fingers in. That night I learned that there are even different ways to roll the ball and little arrows on the floor to help you line it up. Because my team was willing to celebrate my failure, I became open to some coaching. I even got my very first score that night. Sure, it was only a 12, but it was better than my usual zero."

If you can take your team from zero to twelve and beyond, then you are a true leader.

# CONCLUSION

*Start with good people, lay out the rules, communicate with your employees, motivate them and reward them. If you do all those things effectively, you can't miss.*
*~ Lee Iacocca*

This leadership thing isn't easy! It almost seems like it's a thankless job, and yet leaders are lauded wherever you go.

Make yourself laudable: Listen.

Really, it all comes down to effective communication. If you are willing to continually seek this, you will increase your team's effectiveness.

No, you will never master perfect communication with people. If there were a way to permanently master communication skills it would cost millions – if not hundreds of millions – to learn. Luckily, you and I both know that this is an ongoing mission of passion. Never stop learning. Never stop growing. Never stop celebrating.

Your deep desire to be a more effective leader, combined with your willingness to continue to learn and grow, will spur you and your team on to greater and more meaningful successes.

Congratulations, you've taken the vital first step!

# ABOUT THE AUTHOR

A recovering accountant with over 20 years of corporate experience, Mélanie Hope has seen more than her fair share of bad bosses. While in the role of manager all the way up to Controller, she was constantly on the lookout for ways to create the most dynamic teams.

As an award-winning speaker and author, she swapped horror stories with people from all over the world. Using her own experiences, these stories, and years of research, she developed a training program for leaders that enables them to see how much their leadership styles affect the rest of their organizations and what they can do to become more effective.

Mélanie currently teaches workshops on leadership for a major seminar company, as well as delivering keynotes for well-known corporations all over the world.

Her books, *Nose-to-Nose Networking* and *Get Over It & Get Started*, have received international acclaim. She is the author of several other communications and business-related books, including *Improv Your Bottom Line* and *Nose-to-Nose Marketing*.

To book Mélanie for your next event, visit MelanieHope.com

# INDEX

Leadership issues? Communication questions?

*Book Mélanie Hope to speak for your next event.*

## Topics from this book:

- Who & How to Hire and Fire
- Creating that Bullet-Proof Battle Plan to Turn that Employee Around
- Mentoring for the New Millennium

Mélanie will tailor a dynamic presentation or workshop for your business.

Visit melaniehope.com for ideas and details!

Bring all the enthusiasm and honesty to your event!

*Book Mélanie Hope to speak today.*

"*Mélanie has an enthusiastic presence that will help any organization or individual grow. She lights up a room with humor and energy!*"

David Clark, Owner, Chivalry Productions

Paperback ISBN: 9781463742072
Kindle ASIN: B0094KJE5O
getoveritandgetstarted.com

Keynotes based on the principles in her hit book "Get Over It & Get Started" include:

- Own It, Overcome It & Optimize It – Whatever "It" Is
- How to Get Over Your Fear, Failure, and Other Self-Inflicted Nonsense
- Busyness as an excuse to not get busy... and why guilt is stupid

*Check out Mélanie's most popular book & workshops:*

# Nose-to-Nose Networking

**Old-fashioned, in-person networking with intention.**

*"This old dog learned a couple of new tricks. It's a very worthwhile book that everyone can gain something from."*

Bob Ingram, President,
Relationship Strategies University

Paperback ISBN: 9781453721308
Kindle ASIN: B00CKCKIUI
nosetonosenetworking.com

## Keynotes and workshops include:
- Networking with Intention
- Getting Into and Out of Conversations with Style
- Friend-building 101: Overcoming social anxiety